Answe[illegible]
Revision Qu[illegible]
for
Intermediate 2
Chemistry

J M Briggs
(Dalziel High School, Motherwell)

D A Buchanan
(Moray House Institute, Edinburgh University)

J R Melrose
(Lenzie Academy, Lenzie, Glasgow)

CHEMCORD

Published by
Chemcord
Inch Keith
East Kilbride
Glasgow

ISBN 1 870570 76 6

Typeset by J M Briggs
Printed by Bell and Bain Ltd, Glasgow

Contents

Unit 1 - Building Blocks

Unit 2 - Carbon Compounds

Unit 3 - Acids, Bases and Metals

Prescribed Practical Activities

Unit 1

Exercise 1.1 — Elements

1. (a) eg. sodium, iron (b) eg. nitrogen, fluorine
   (c) eg, sulphur,magnesium (d) mercury, bromine
   (e) eg. chlorine, argon (f) eg. sodium, chlorine
   (g) eg. gold, silver (h) eg. einsteinium, fermium

2. (a) 105
   (b) (i) a vertical column of the Periodic Table
   (ii) a horizontal row of the Periodic Table

3. (a) (i) vanadium (ii) lithium (iii) argon (iv) nickel
   (v) chlorine (vi) potassium (vii) neon (viii) fluorine
   (b) (i) chlorine, fluorine (ii) lithium, potassium
   (iii) vanadium, nickel (iv) argon, neon
   (c) (i) They are very reactive with water (an alkali and hydrogen are formed).
   (ii) They are very unreactive.

4. (a) (i) Na (ii) He (iii) Al
   (iv) C (v) Pb (vi) Ga
   (b) aluminium, gallium

5. They are both in Group 4 of the Periodic Table.

6. (a) eg. sodium, Na (b) eg. phosphorus, P
   (c) chlorine, Cl (d) carbon, C
   (e) tungsten, W (f) argon, Ar
   (g) hydrogen, H (h) helium, He
   (i) nitrogen, N (j) oxygen, O
   (k) eg. plutonium, Pu (l) eg. europium, Eu
   (m) californium, Cf (n) einsteinium, Es
   (o) nobelium, No (p) curium, Cm

Exercise 1.2 Compounds and mixtures

1. (a) (i) An element is a substance made up of only one kind of atom.
(ii) A compound is a substance made up of two or more kinds of atom, joined by a chemical reaction.
(b) (i) No, because the element contains only one kind of atom.
(ii) Yes, because it is possible to separate the different kinds of atom.
(c) sodium sulphite, sugar, salt, copper chloride.

2. Elements carbon, zinc, oxygen, gold, nitrogen, aluminium.
Compounds petrol, alcohol, sugar, sodium chloride, copper sulphate, silver oxide.

3. Elements mentioned
oxygen, carbon, hydrogen, iron, zinc, copper, gold, (coal - impure carbon)
Compounds mentioned
glucose, carbon dioxide, water, starch, (gas , petrol - mixtures of compounds)

4. (a) (i) magnesium chloride (ii) lead sulphide
(iii) sodium oxide (iv) hydrogen iodide
(b) potassium sulphite, potassium sulphate.

5. (a) **W** - oxygen, **X** - magnesium oxide, **Y** - carbon
(b) The concentration of oxygen (20%) is too low.

6.

Formula of substance	Element	Compound	Elements present
$CaSO_3$	no	yes	calcium, sulphur, oxygen
He	yes	no	helium
NaBr	no	yes	sodium, bromine
LiCl	no	yes	lithium, chlorine
ZnI_2	no	yes	zinc, iodine
Fe	yes	no	iron
KNO_3	no	yes	potassium, nitrogen, oxygen
Xe	yes	no	xenon
I_2	yes	no	iodine
$BaSO_4$	no	yes	barium, sulphur, oxygen
Sn	yes	no	tin
HCl	no	yes	hydrogen, chlorine
Hg	yes	no	mercury
As	yes	no	arsenic
$MgCO_3$	no	yes	magnesium, carbon, oxygen

7. (a) an element
   (b) The iron has joined with the sulphur to form a compound, iron sulphide.

8. (a) A substance made up of two or more elements or compounds which can be separated by physical methods.
   (b) (i) air, milk, soil
       (ii) iron, oxygen, water, carbon dioxide

9. (a) (i) A substance which dissolves in a liquid.
       (ii) A liquid in which a solid dissolves.
       (iii) A mixture made by dissolving a solid, liquid or gas in a liquid until no more will dissolve.
   (b) (i) ethanoic acid
       (ii) water
       (iii) vinegar
   (c)

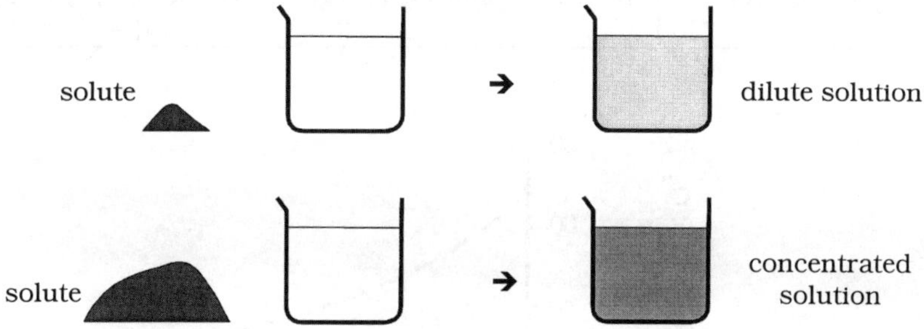

10.

State symbol	Meaning
(s)	solid
(l)	liquid
(g)	gas
(aq)	dissolved in water

11. (a) oxygen
    (b) **X** must contain oxygen.

12. (a) (i) oxygen
        (ii) The minimum volume of gas in the apparatus is approximately 80%, suggesting that 20% of the air has been used. This is the approximate percentage of oxygen in air.
    (b) The rate of reaction decreased as oxygen was used up.

13. Oxygen from the air would allow the fat used to prepare the crisps to turn sour because of the effect of bacteria. Unreactive nitrogen replaces this.

14.

Use of chlorine	Percentage / %
PVC	27
Solvents	16
Aerosol propellant	17
Chemicals	14
Other uses	26

15.

Type	Composition	Example
bromide	100% silver bromide	Brovira, Pal
bromo-chloride	60% silver bromide,40% silver chloride	Galerie, Oriental, Elite
chloro-bromide	60% silver chloride,40% silver bromide	Record-Rapid, Portriga

16. (a)

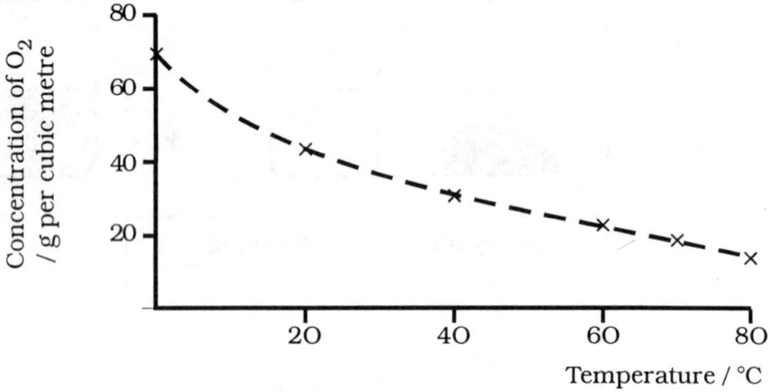

(b) 54 g dissolved oxygen per cubic metre

(c) 53 °C

17. (a)

Constituents of glass	Mass
sand	200 g
sodium carbonate	150 g
calcium carbonate	50 g

(b) Constituents of glass

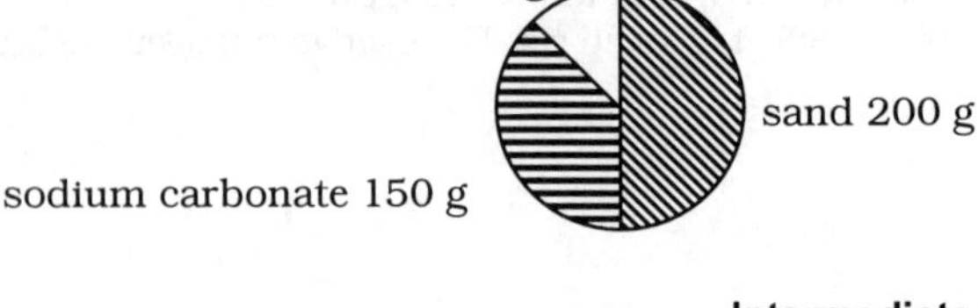

18. (a)

Light passing through / %

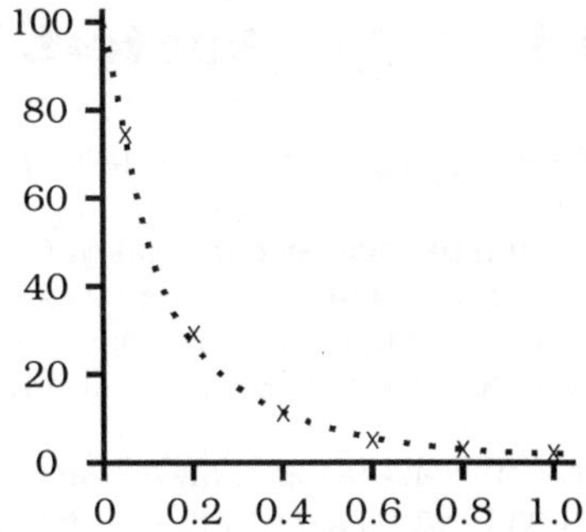

Concentration of $CuSO_4$ / mol per litre

(b) The greater the concentration of the copper sulphate solution the smaller the percentage of light passing through.
(c) 0.1 mol per litre

19. (a) cellulose (b) react with sulphite solution

Exercise 1.3 Chemical reactions

1. (a) In a chemical reaction at least one new substance forms.
   (b) (i), (iv), (vi), (vii), (ix)

2. (a) Sodium goes on fire, white solid forms (heat energy is released).
   (b) The coal flame, solid turns to gas (heat energy is released).
   (c) Magnesium breaks up, gas is given off (heat energy is released).

3. (a) In an exothermic reaction heat energy is given out to the surroundings.
   (b) In an endothermic reaction heat energy is taken in from the surroundings.

4. (a) Fire - heat energy is given out.
   Colour change - from red-brown (copper) to yellow.
   (b) copper chloride

5. Heat energy is given out.
   The colourless crystals react with the grey powder to give a new substance which is black in colour.

Exercise 1.4 Factors affecting reaction rate

1. match igniting > egg frying > milk turning sour > motor car rusting

2. (a) Decreasing particle size increases reaction rate.
   (b) Increase in concentration increases reaction rate.
   (c) Increase in temperature increases reaction rate.
   (d) Use of a catalyst increases reaction rate.

3. (a) (i) **B** will react faster than **A** due to a decrease in particle size.
   (ii) **A** will react faster than **C** due to a decrease in concentration of the acid.
   (b) The rate of reaction would increase due to the increase in temperature.

4. (a) Flame temperature increases.
   (b) Increase in concentration of oxygen increases reaction rate and heat energy is produced faster.

5. (a) a match igniting, etc.
   (b) epoxy glue setting, etc.
   (c) iron nails going rusty, etc.

6. The spray of petrol consists of tiny droplets. This increases the surface area of petrol at which combustion occurs.

7. (a) Smaller particle size; speeds up reaction.
   (b) Increases oxygen concentration; speeds up reaction.
   (c) Decreases temperature; slows down reaction.
   (d) Increase of temperature; speeds up reaction.
   (e) Increase of particle size; slows down reaction.
   (f) Increase in concentration of oxygen; speeds up reaction.

8. (a) Volume of gas would be greater.
   (b) 40 cm^3 (mass of calcium carbonate unchanged)

9. (a) 49 cm^3
   (b) (i) Slope of graph is less.
   (ii) lower temperature, larger marble chips
   (c) Final volume of carbon dioxide produced is the same.

10. (a) 27 cm^3
   (b) 5 s
   (c) 30 cm^3
   (d)

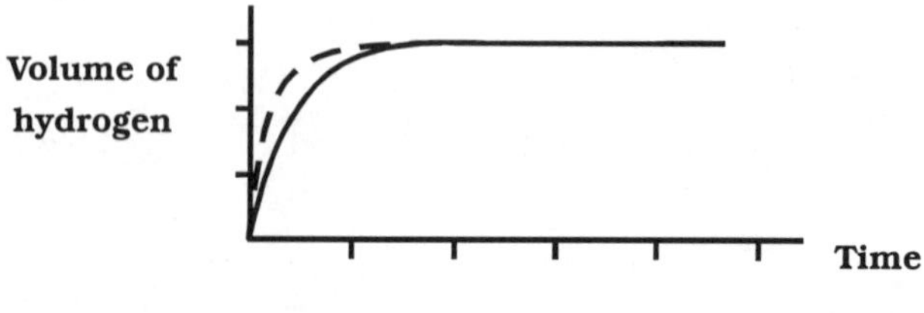

11. (a) **X**
(b) mass of calcium carbonate, volume and concentration of acid, temperature

12. (a) **C** < **A** < **B**
(b) The concentration of acid in **B** is double that in **A**. This will liberate twice the volume of carbon dioxide and double the mass lost.

13.

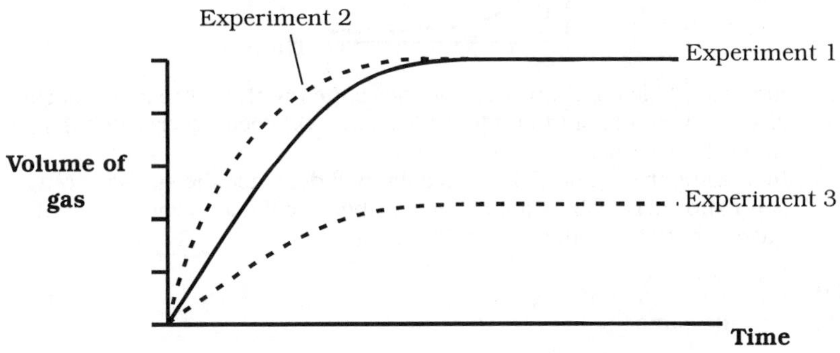

14. (a) The reaction gives out heat energy. The increase in temperature of the reactants causes the reaction rate to increase.
(b) Hydrogen is given off and lost to the atmosphere.

15.

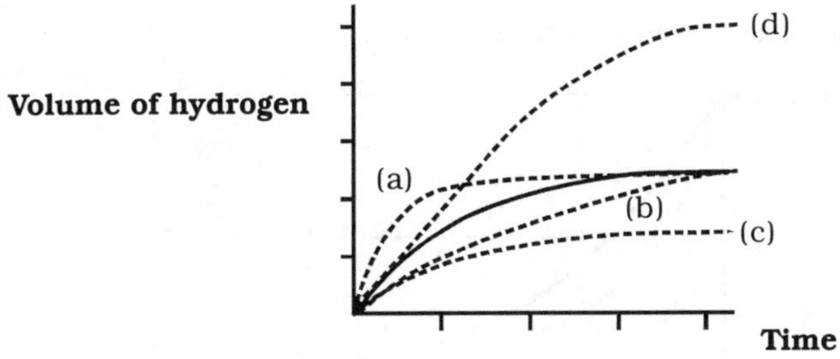

16. (a) (i) $Mg(s) + 2HCl(aq) \rightarrow MgCl_2(aq) + H_2(g)$
(ii) $Zn(s) + 2HCl(aq) \rightarrow ZnCl_2(aq) + H_2(g)$
(iii) $2Na(s) + 2HCl(aq) \rightarrow 2NaCl(aq) + H_2(g)$

(b)

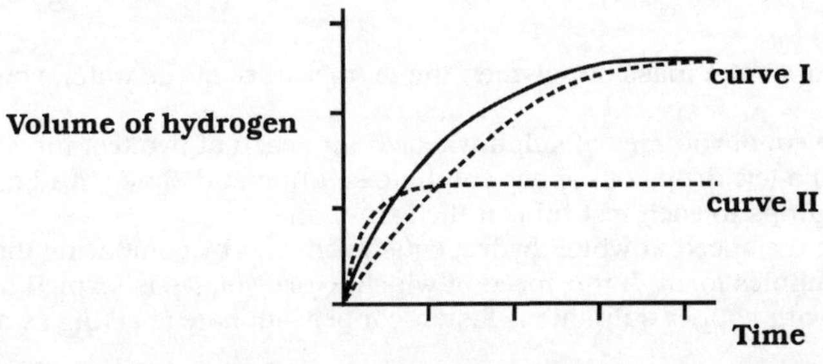

17.

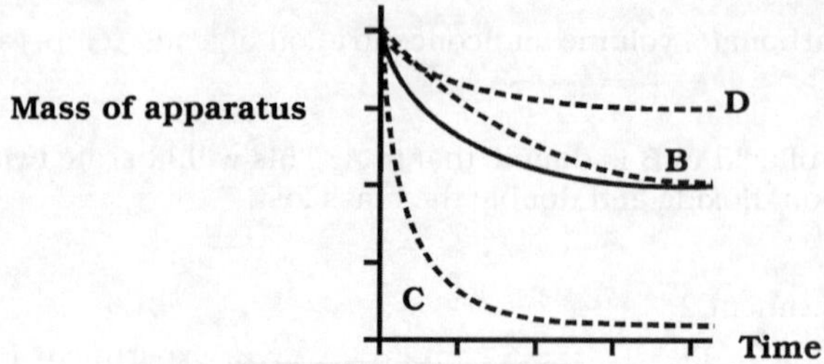

18. (a) Increasing the concentration increases the number of reactant particles in a given volume of solution. More collisions will occur, therefore the reaction rate will increase.
    (b) Increasing the particle size of a solid will decrease the surface area of the solid and there will be a smaller number of collisions with reactant particles. The reaction rate will decrease.

19. (a) increase
    (b) stay the same

20. (a) 50 min (b) sample **A** (c) sample **B**

21. (a) The concentration of iodate ions in solution.
    (b) (i) The concentration of sulphite ions in solution.
    (ii) The higher the concentration of sulphite ions, the faster the reaction.

22. (a) Hydrogen produced is lost to the atmosphere.
    (b)

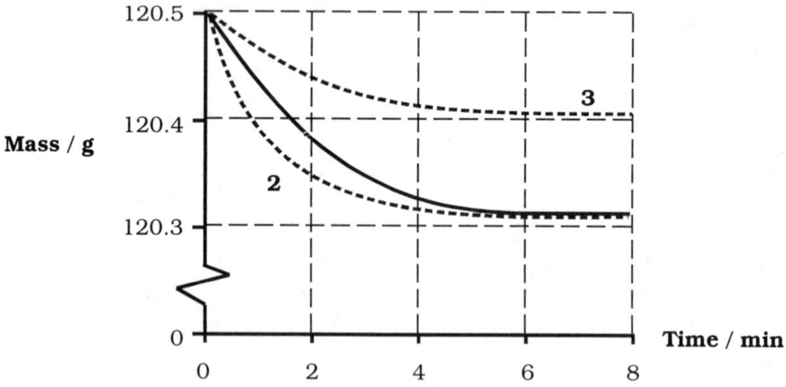

23. For example, the mass of polymer, the temperature of the water, volume of water.

24. Measure equal volumes of sulphuric acid into each of two test tubes. To one test tube add a few drops of copper sulphate solution and shake. Add equal masses of zinc lumps to each test tube at the same time.
Measure the speed at which hydrogen is produced by comparing the rate at which bubbles form. If the speed at which hydrogen gas is formed in the test tube treated with copper sulphate is faster, copper sulphate is acting as a catalyst.

25.

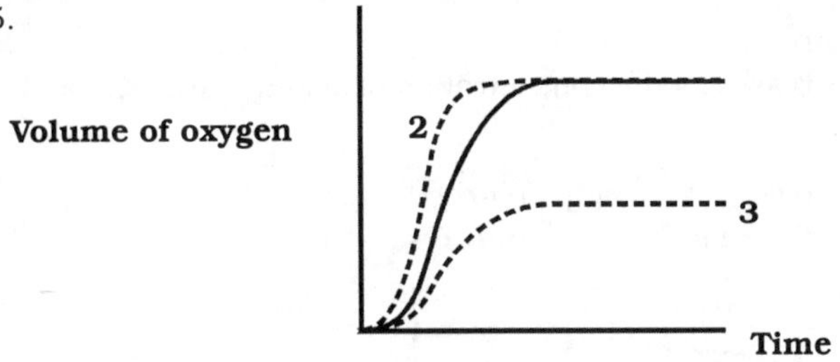

26. (a) Volume of water and temperature are the same.
    (b) How the speed of dissolving varies with temperature.

27. Place 2 ice cubes in the filter funnel and allow them to melt at room temperature. Collect the water in the measuring cylinder and find the time required for 10 cm^3 of water to form.
    Repeat the experiment but sprinkle salt on the 2 ice cubes before measuring the time required for 10 cm^3 of water to form.

Exercise 1.5 Following the course of a reaction

1.

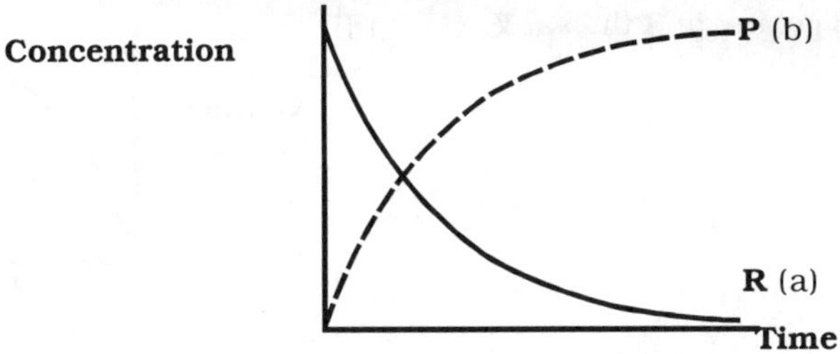

    (c) The steeper the gradient, the faster the reaction.

2. (a) (i) 0.1 mol $l^{-1}min^{-1}$ (ii) 0.06 mol $l^{-1}min^{-1}$ (iii) 0.035 mol $l^{-1}min^{-1}$
   (b) (i) The reaction rate decreases.
       (ii) As the reaction proceeds the concentration of reactant decreases.

3. (a) One of the products is a gas.
   (b)

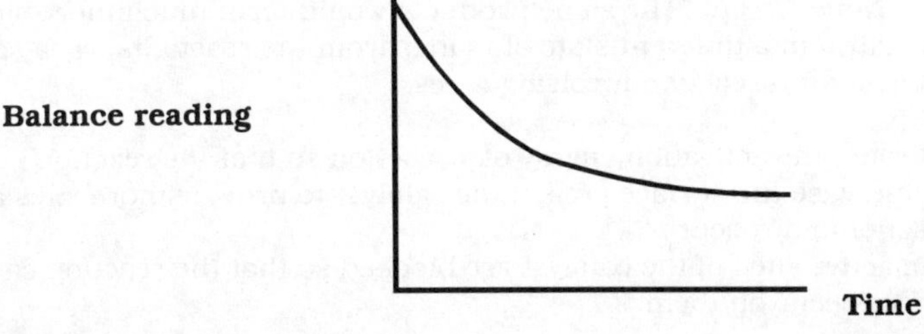

4. (a) $72\ cm^3$
(b) i) 75 s ii) 20 s
(iii) The reaction rate decreases as the concentration of acid decreases.
(c) $1.9\ cm^3\ s^{-1}$

5. (a) 12 s (b) 10 °C (c) $0.66\ s^{-1}$
(d) (i) 25 s (ii) 12 s (iii) 6 s

6.

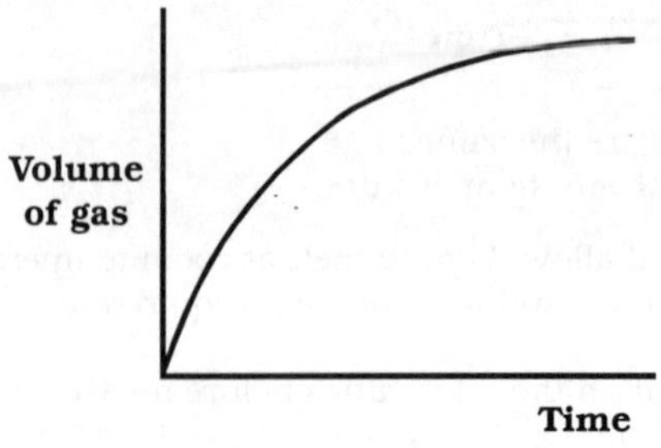

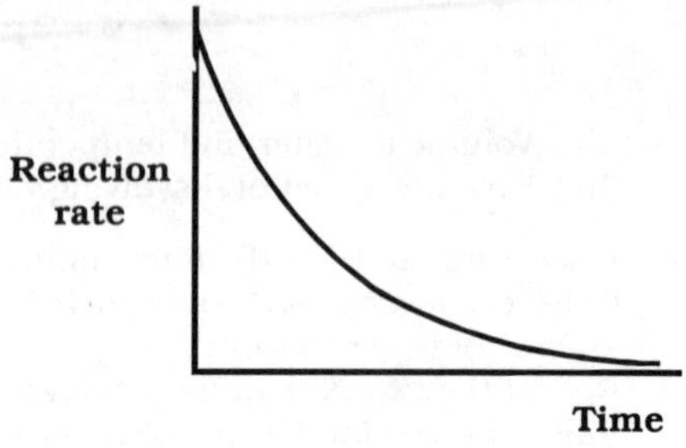

7. (a) $0.0095\ mol\ l^{-1}$ (b) $9 \times 10^{-6}\ mol\ l^{-1}\ s^{-1}$
(c) As the reaction proceeds, the concentration of methyl ethanoate and hydroxide ions falls and the reaction rate decreases.

8. (a) The rate is greater at **X** than at **Y**.
(b) $0.3\ g\ min^{-1}$
(c) 3.5 min
(d)

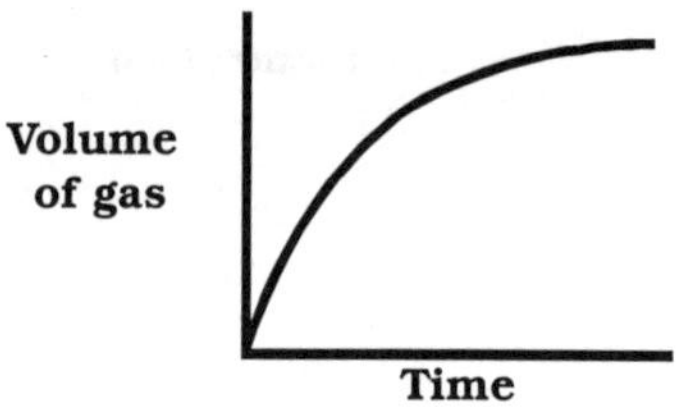

Exercise 1.6 Catalysts

1. (a) A catalyst increases the rate of a reaction but remains chemically unchanged at the end of the reaction.
(b) There would be no change of mass.

2. (a) (i) To increase the surface area of the catalyst so that the reaction is faster.
(ii) nitrogen and water
Note: Accept "The same products would form much more slowly."
(b) A catalyst in a different state of matter from the reactants, eg. a solid catalyst for a reaction involving gases.

3. (a) It lowers the activation energy of a reaction so that the reaction is faster.
(b) To increase the surface area of the catalyst to provide more sites at which a reaction may occur.
(c) The active sites of the catalyst are blocked so that the reaction can no longer occur on them.

4. (a) The reaction between sodium potassium tartrate and hydrogen peroxide is possible without a catalyst.
The green colour shows that cobalt chloride is taking part in the reaction, i.e. is acting as a catalyst, which allows the reaction to proceed faster. When one of the reactants is used up, the colour changes back to pink indicating that the original cobalt chloride has reformed and is therefore unchanged at the end of the reaction.
(b) homogeneous

5. (a) enzymes
(b) For example, the fermentation of glucose to ethanol and carbon dioxide using zymase.

6.

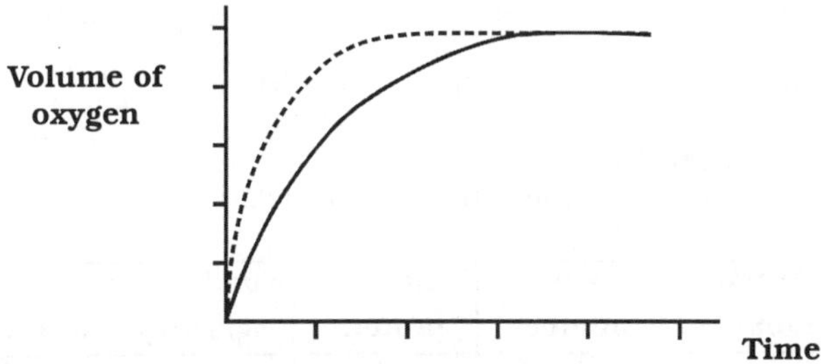

7. (a) To increase the surface area of the catalyst and speed up the reaction further.
(b) heterogeneous
(c) The conversion of carbon monoxide to carbon dioxide or of nitrogen oxides to nitrogen.
(d) Lead is deposited on the surface of the catalyst and poisons it.

8. (a) For example, iron in the Haber process.
(b) For example, zymase used to catalyse the fermentation of glucose.

9. Shape **D**, because it has the largest surface area for the size of the pellet.

Exercise 1.7 The structure of the atom

1. (a) (i) nucleus (ii) positive
(b) (i) electrons (ii) negative
(c) The number of protons is equal to the number of electrons.

2. (a) vanadium (b) lithium (c) argon (d) nickel
(e) chlorine (f) potassium (g) neon (h) fluorine

3.

Particle	Mass	Charge	Location
electron	0	negative 1	outside nucleus
proton	1 amu	positive 1	nucleus
neutron	1 amu	0	nucleus

4. (a) sodium (b) neon (c) aluminium
(d) carbon (e) fluorine (f) silicon

5. (a) chlorine (b) sodium (c) carbon (d) oxygen

6. (a) (i) The number of protons in the nucleus of an atom.
(ii) The total number of protons and neutrons in the nucleus of an atom.
(b) (i) **x** is the mass number of potassium.
(ii) **y** is the atomic number of potassium.

7. (a) 11p, 12n, 11e (b) 8p, 8n, 8e (c) 1p, 2n, 1e
(d) 17p, 18n, 17e (e) 1p, 0n, 1e (f) 20p, 20n, 20e
(g) 19p, 20n, 19e (h) 3p, 4n, 3e (i) 16p, 16n, 16e

8. (a) ^{18}O (b) ^{13}C (c) ^{37}Cl (d) ^{3}H

9. 2 protons, 2 neutrons, 0 electrons
(the alpha particle is a positive ion with a charge of 2+)

10.

Element	Atomic number	Mass number	Number of protons	Number of neutrons	Number of electrons
Ne	10	22	10	12	10
N	7	14	7	7	7
Ca	20	40	20	20	20
A	4	9	4	5	4
B	6	14	6	8	6
C	36	89	36	53	36
D	10	20	10	10	10
E	15	32	15	17	15

(b) **A** - beryllium, **B** - carbon, **C** - krypton, **D** - neon, **E** - phosphorus

11. (a) Atoms of the same element with different numbers of neutrons.
(b) They must be equal.

12. (a) They have different numbers of neutrons in their nuclei.
(b) They have the same number of protons and electrons, and therefore behave chemically in the same ways.
(c) The relative proportions of the isotopes in a sample of neon.

13. (a) (i) 1 (ii) 0 (iii) mass number
(b) (i) 1 (ii) 1 (iii) It has the same atomic number but has a heavier nucleus.
(c) isotopes

14. (a) isotopes
(b) There are many more ^{7}Li atoms (90%) than there are ^{6}Li atoms (10%).

15. (a) 93
(b) 145
(c) (i) no
(ii) Different numbers of protons in their nuclei.

16. (a) ^{63}Cu - 34 neutrons, ^{65}Cu - 36 neutrons
(b) ^{63}Cu is more abundant.

17. (a) There must be a greater number of protons in the new nucleus.
(b) hydrogen (the only element with a lighter nucleus than helium)

Exercise 1.8 The Periodic Table

1. (a) a solid
(b) Reacts vigorously with water.

2. Effectiveness in reducing "pinking" increases going down a group and decreases from Group 6 to Group 7.
Hence lead, at the bottom of Group 4, should be very effective in reducing pinking.

3. (a) Use the same number of drops of sodium sulphate solution.
Use the same volumes of solutions 1, 2, 3 and 4.
Ensure that all are at the same temperature.
(b) calcium sulphate
(c) no solid

4. (a) The iron wool glows very brightly even when the heat is removed.
(b) iron fluoride

5. (a) using electricity
(b) The further to the left of the Periodic Table a metal is, the more difficult it is to extract.

6. (a) Halogens higher in Group 7 will displace halogens lower in the group from solutions of their halide salts.
(b) no reaction

7. (a) (i) **C**
(ii) **B**
(iii) **A**
(b) (i) vs (ii) i

Exercise 1.9 Bonding and structure

1. (a) A fixed number of atoms held together by covalent bonds.
   (b) A shared pair of electrons joining atoms together.
   (c) A way of stating, using atomic symbols, the number of atoms of each kind of element present in a molecule of a substance.

2. (a) A diatomic molecule consists of 2 atoms joined by covalent bonding.
   (b) (iii), (v), (vii), (x), (xi)

3. (a)

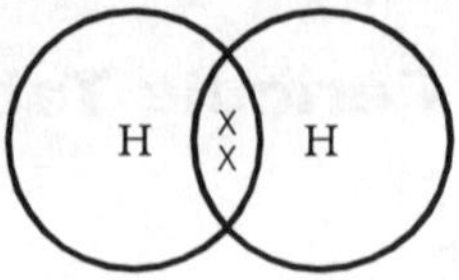

(b)

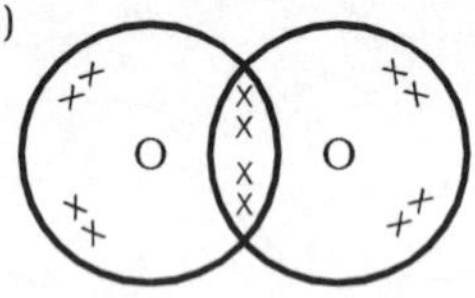

(c)

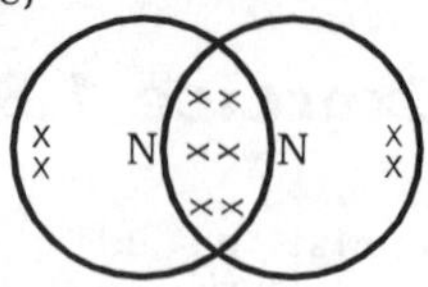

(d)

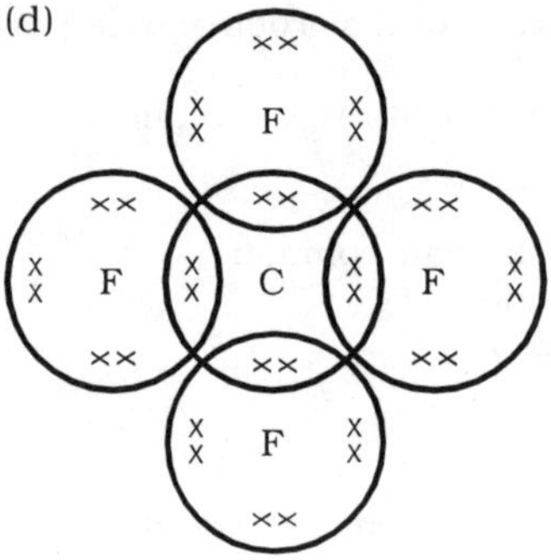

(e)

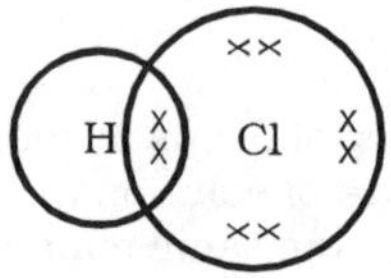

(f)

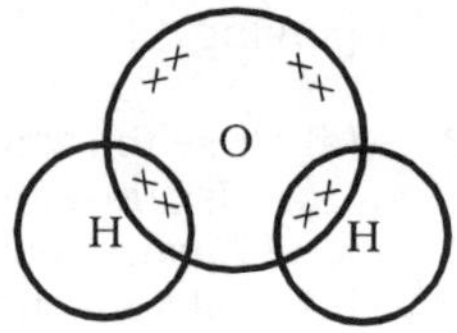

(g)

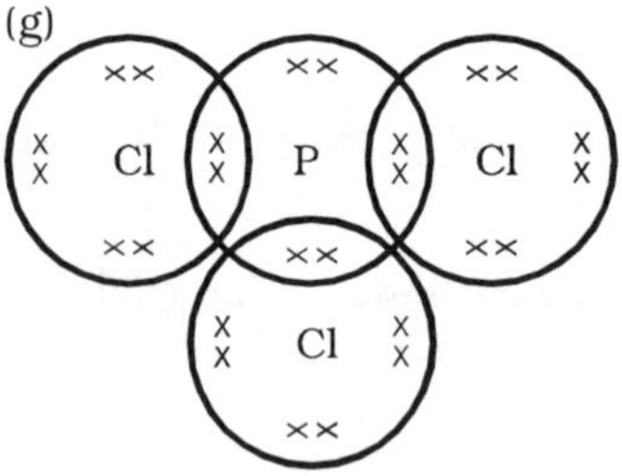

(h)

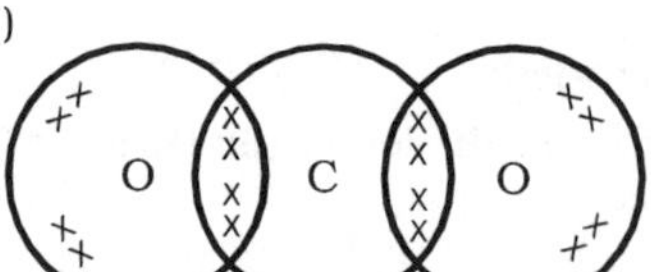

4. (a) Both electrons in the overlapping region of the outermost shells are attracted to each hydrogen nucleus by electrostatic forces causing the two nuclei to be held together. This more than compensates for the additional repulsive force between the two electrons and makes the molecule more stable than the individual atoms.

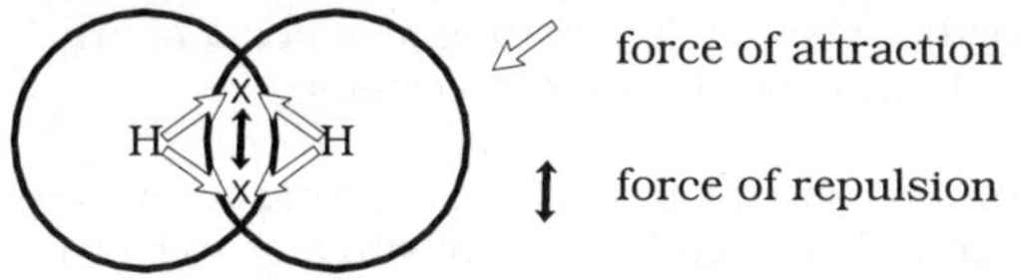

(b) The strength of bonds between different moleculesis usually very small compared with the strength of the covalent bonds within a molecule.

5. (i)

(ii)

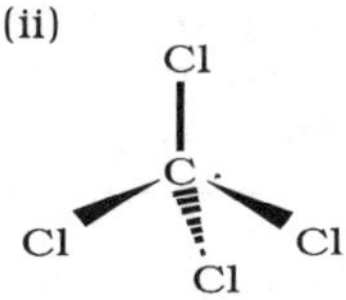

(iii)

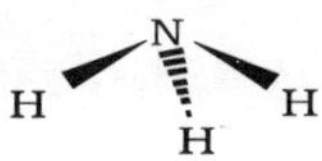

(iv)

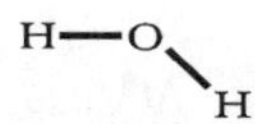

(b) (i) nitrogen
(ii) water
(c) tetrahedral

6.

Covalent bonding	Ionic bonding	Metallic bonding
hydrogen chloride	sodium chloride	copper
carbon sulphide	aluminium nitrate	mercury
phosphorus oxide	iron oxide	Al
oxygen	copper sulphate	Na
CH_3Cl	MgO	
NO_2	$FeCl_2$	
Cl_2	Na_2CO_3	
C_2H_5OH		
$C_6H_{12}O_6$		

7. (a) The density is equal to the relative atomic mass.
(b) 65.5

8. (a) Because oxygen has a much stronger attraction for the bonding electrons than hydrogen has, the electrons are drawn closer to the oxygen atom in the molecule, polarising the bond.
(b) For example, hydrogen, nitrogen, oxygen.

9. (a) Discrete molecules contain a fixed number of atoms held together by covalent bonds.
   (b) A covalent network structure is a three-dimensional lattice in which a very large number of atoms is held together by covalent bonds.

10. Copper is held together by metallic bonding in which a network of positive ions is held together by a delocalised "sea" of electrons.

11. (a) (i) The outermost energy level of the chlorine atom gains an electron to become complete, forming an ion with a charge of 1–.
   (ii) The outermost energy level of the calcium atom loses two electrons to leave a complete third energy level, forming an ion with a charge of 2+.
   (b) The electrostatic attracton of the positively charged calcium ions attracts chloride ions from every direction to become surrounded by chloride ion nearest neighbours. In turn, the chloride ions attract calcium ions so that a three-dimensional lattice forms containing calcium ions and chloride ions in the ratio 1:2.

12. (a)

Ion	Number of protons	Number of electrons
Ca^{2+}	20	18
Cl^{-}	17	18
Al^{3+}	13	10
O^{2-}	8	10

   (b) (i) Zn^{2+} (ii) Cu^{+} (iii) S^{2-} (iv) Sn^{2+}

13. **Transfer of one electron**

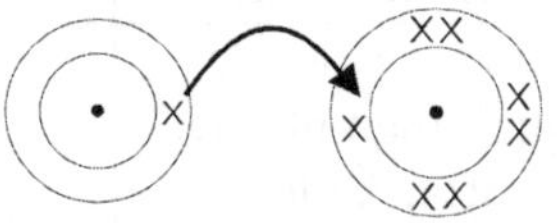

14. (a) A lattice consists of a three-dimensional array of positive and negative ions in which the positive ions are surrounded by negatively charged nearest neighbours and vice versa.
   (b) A molecule consists of a fixed number of atoms held together by covalent bonds. In sodium chloride, the bonding is ionic and a lattice forms, consisting of an indeterminate number of positive and negative ions.

15. Sulphur trioxide exists as small molecules each of which contains 1 sulphur atom and 3 oxygen atoms.
Magnesium chloride is made up of a three-dimensional array containing magnesium ions surrounded by chloride ions and vice versa. The ratio of magnesium ions to chloride ions is 1:2.
Silicon dioxide is made up of a three-dimensional network containing silicon atoms joined by covalent bonds to four oxygen atoms. These tetrahedra join so that the ratio of silicon atoms to oxygen atoms is 1:2.

Exercise 1.10 Properties

1. (a)

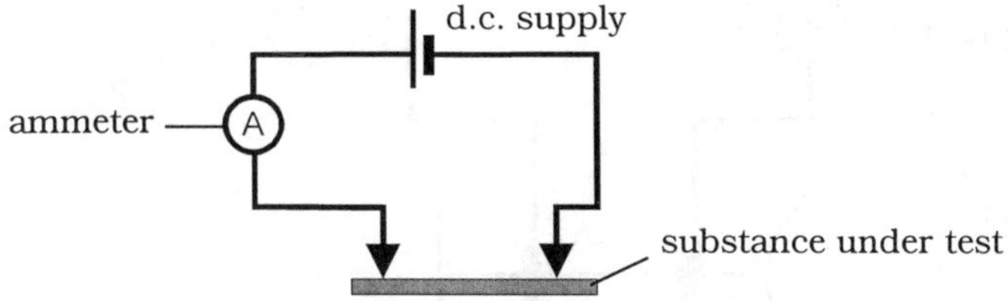

(b)

Conductors	Non-conductors
nickel copper magnesium sodium scandium	iodine sulphur phosphorus

(c)

Conductors	Non-conductors
copper sulphate solution molten iron sodium chloride solution mercury strontium nitrate solution	petrol silicon tetrachloride hexene liquid oxygen molten sulphur

2. (a) silver, potassium
   (b) (i) sodium bromide, nickel chloride
   (ii) Their ions are not free to move in the solid state.

3. (a) **B** (b) **A** (c) **C**

4. (a) **P** - glucose, **Q** - aluminium, **R** - copper bromide, **S** - sodium chloride
   (b) **P** - covalent, **R** - ionic, **S** - ionic
   (c) (i) **Q** is a metal and has delocalised electrons which are free to move in the solid state.
   (ii) In the solid state ions of **R** and **S** are not free to move.
   In the molten state ions of **R** and **S** are free to move.

5. a)

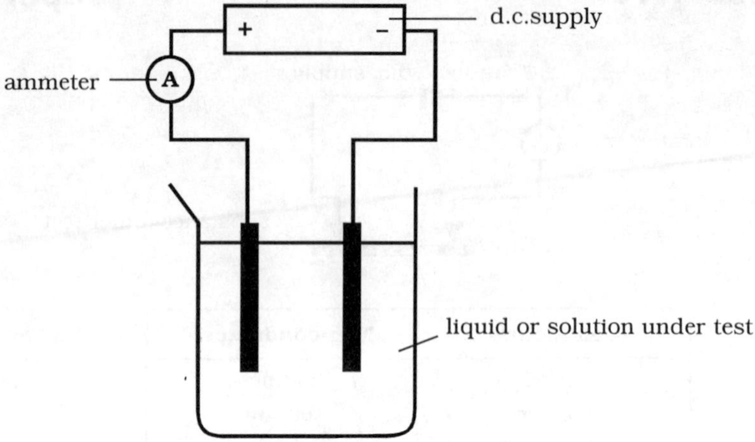

(b) (i) **X**Cl - ionic, $\mathbf{Y}Cl_4$ - covalent
(ii) Group 1

6. (a) **Q** and **R**
(b) **Q** and **R**

7. **A** - covalent network; does not conduct, high melting point
B - covalent small molecules; does not conduct, low melting point
C - ionic; high melting point, conducts when molten and in solution

8. (a) Sodium oxide is an ionic compound. All its ions are held together in a lattice by strong ionic bonds which require much energy to break, so high temperatures are needed to make the compound melt.
(b) Carbon monoxide exists as small molecules which are only very weakly attracted to each other. The boiling point is lower than room temperature beause little energy is needed to separate the molecules.
(c) Silicon dioxide forms a network covalent lattice in which all atoms are held together by very strong covalent bonds which require much energy to break, giving a high melting point.

9. (a) sodium
(b) They are negatively charged.
(c) Different samples contain different quantities and types of dissolved minerals depending on the ground over which the water has collected. Different types and concentrations of different ions will give different conductivities.

10. (a) In air, sodium or magnesium would catch fire when heated. Argon is an inert gas.
(b) Titanium(IV) chloride is covalent.

11. **P** Covalent network, because it does not conduct and has unusually high melting and boiling points.
Q Metallic, because it can condust in the solid state.
R Ionic, because it can conduct when molten or in solution.
S Discrete molecular, because it does not conduct and has low melting and boiling points.

Exercise 1.11 Electrolysis

1. (a) The breaking down of a compound by the passage of a current of electricity through a solution or a melt.
(b) (i) magnesium - negative electrode; chlorine - positive electrode
(ii) sodium - negative electrode; iodine - positive electrode
(iii) lead - negative electrode; bromine - positive electrode
(iv) calcium - negative electrode; oxygen - positive electrode

2. (a) Cadmium iodide is an ionic compound and conducts in molten state but not in solid state.
(b) cadmium - negative electrode; iodine - positive electrode
(c) Both electrodes touch the nickel crucible, or sufficient cadmium metal has been produced to allow conduction between electrodes.

3. (a) electrolysis
(b) chlorine
(c) Positive copper ions are attracted to the negative electrode, gain electrons and become copper metal atoms. Copper metal is brown.

4. (a)

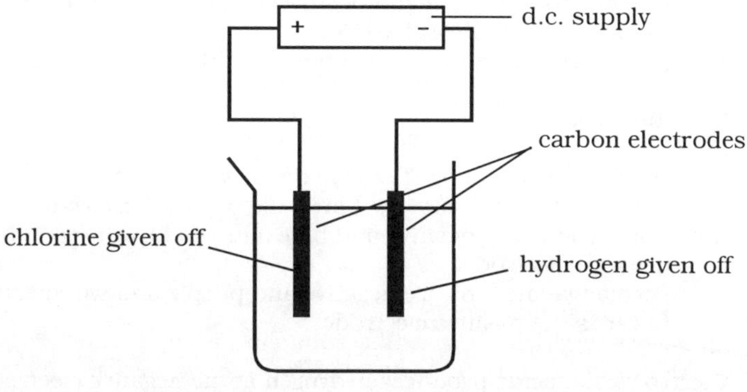

(b) Hydrochloric acid contains chloride ions which are negatively charged and are attracted towards the positive electrode.
(c) The electrodes would react with the hydrochloric acid.

5. (a) If the mixture solidified, aluminium and oxide ions would be unable to move.
(b) Aluminium ions are positively charged and will move towards the negative electrode where they gain electrons to form atoms of aluminium metal.

6. (a) So that the direction of movement of the ions in the solution is not constantly being reversed.
   (b) The electrode would be coated by a silvery deposit of nickel because Ni^{2+} ions are attracted to the electrode and gain electrons to become nickel atoms.
   (c) A brown solution of bromine would form since Br^- ions are attracted to the electrode, lose electrons and form bromine molecules.
   (d) It is a covalent substance and will not conduct electricity because no ions are present.

7. (a) Solid sodium chloride does not conduct since its ions are not free to move.
   (b) (i) positive electrode
   (ii) chloride ions, Cl^-, are attracted to the positive electrode and lose electrons to form chlorine atoms. These join to form diatomic chlorine molecules, Cl_2.

8. (a) (i) glucose (ii) covalent
   (b) silver nitrate
   (c) chlorine

9. (a) blue (b) violet (c) green

10. (a) (i) The dichromate ion is orange and negatively charged.
   (ii) The ion is attracted towards the positive electrode and must therefore be negatively charged and is orange in colour.
   (b) Ensure that there is no contact between the operator and the appareatus when the current is switched on.

11. (a) (i) Green colour will move towards the negative electrode.
   (ii) Nickel ions are green and positively charged and will be attracted towards the negative elctrode.
   (b) The green band will move in the opposite direction.

12. (a) It conducts electricity.
   (b) purple
   (c) (i) Blue colour will move towards the negative electrode.
   Purple colour will move towards the positive electrode.
   (ii) Copper ions are positive and blue and will be attracted to the negative electrode.
   Permanganate ions are negative and purple and will be attracted towards the positive electrode.

13. (a) Electrolysis of acids produces hydrogen at the negative electrode.
   (b) Hydrogen - negative electrode; oxygen - positive electrode.
   (c) Potassium chloride is an ionic compound. In the solid state, its ions are not free to move, but are able to move freely in solution, hence the solution conducts electricity but the solid does not.

14. (a) an electrolyte
   (b) temperature, depth of immersion of electrodes, nature of electrodes
   (c) The lower the concentration, the smaller the conductivity.
   (d) hydrochloric acid> sodium hydroxide> sodium chloride

Exercise 1.12 Formulae (i)

1. (a) Cl_2O (b) H_2 (c) C_2H_4 (d) C_6H_6O (e) C_3H_6O

2. (a) hydrogen chloride (b) nitrogen (c) carbon chloride
   (d) nitrogen hydride (e) hydrogen oxide
   (f) oxygen (g) chlorine

3. (a) SO_3 (b) CO_2 (c) CO (d) SiF_4 (e) PCl_5 (f) UF_6

Exercise 1.13 Formulae (ii)

1. (a) H_2O (b) PF_3 (c) NCl_3 (d) HI (e) SCl_2 (f) SiO_2

2. (a) NaBr (b) KCl (c) $MgCl_2$
   (d) CaS (e) Al_2O_3 (f) MgO
   (g) LiOH (h) K_2SO_4 (i) $CsNO_3$
   (j) K_2CO_3 (k) $SrSO_4$ (l) NH_4Cl

3. (a) $Ca(OH)_2$ (b) $Ba(NO_3)_2$ (c) $Mg(NO_3)_2$
   (d) $(NH_4)_2SO_4$ (e) $Ca(NO_3)_2$ (f) $Al(OH)_3$

4. (a) $PbBr_2$ (b) Cu_2O (c) $FeCl_2$
   (d) $NiSO_4$ (e) $FeCO_3$ (f) $Cu(OH)_2$
   (g) $AgNO_3$ (h) V_2O_5

5. (a) NaCl (b) CO (c) $Mg(OH)_2$
   (d) HCl (e) O_2 (f) $FeCl_3$
   (g) KOH (h) Na (i) NH_4Br
   (j) H_2 (k) RbF (l) SCl_2
   (m) $MgSO_4$ (n) $(NH_4)_2CO_3$ (o) Fe
   (p) CuO (q) Na_2S (r) HF

6. (a) aluminium potassium sulphate (b) $FeNH_4(SO_4)_2$

Exercise 1.14 Equations (i)

1. (a) (i) and (iii) (b) (ii), (iii) and (iv)
   (c) (i) and (ii) (d) (v) and (vi)

2. (a) magnesium + oxygen → magnesium oxide
(b) iron oxide + carbon monoxide → iron + carbon dioxide
(c) starch + water → glucose
(d) calcium + water → calcium hydroxide + hydrogen
(e) copper carbonate → copper oxide + carbon dioxide

3. (b) Carbon monoxide gas reacts with oxygen gas to give carbon dioxide gas.
(c) Carbon solid reacts with chlorine gas to give carbon tetrachloride liquid.
(d) Hydrogen gas reacts with fluorine gas to give hydrogen fluoride gas.
(e) Sulphur dioxide gas reacts with oxygen gas to give sulphur trioxide gas.
(f) Copper oxide solid reacts with carbon monoxide gas to give copper solid and carbon dioxide gas.
(g) Ammonia gas reacts with oxygen gas to give nitrogen gas and hydrogen gas.
(h) Methane gas reacts with oxygen gas to give carbon dioxide gas and water.
(i) Hydrogen bromide gas decomposes to give hydrogen gas and bromine liquid.

Exercise 1.15 Equations (ii)

1. (a) $C + O_2 \rightarrow CO$
(b) $S + O_2 \rightarrow SO_2$
(c) $HCl \rightarrow H_2 + Cl_2$
(d) $N_2 + O_2 \rightarrow NO_2$
(e) $P + Cl_2 \rightarrow PCl_3$

2. (a) $Ca + O_2 \rightarrow CaO$
(b) $Na + Cl_2 \rightarrow NaCl$
(c) $Mg + H_2SO_4 \rightarrow MgSO_4 + H_2$
(d) $Mg + CO_2 \rightarrow MgO + C$
(e) $BaCl_2 + Na_2SO_4 \rightarrow NaCl + BaSO_4$
(f) $CaCO_3 + HCl \rightarrow CaCl_2 + CO_2 + H_2O$

3. (a) $H_2 + O_2 \rightarrow H_2O$
(b) $Na + H_2O \rightarrow NaOH + H_2$
(c) $Si + Cl_2 \rightarrow SiCl_4$
(d) $Ag_2O \rightarrow Ag + O_2$
(e) $C_2H_4 + O_2 \rightarrow CO_2 + H_2O$
(f) $H_2 + I_2 \rightarrow HI$
(g) $Mg + O_2 \rightarrow MgO$
(h) $NH_3 \rightarrow N_2 + H_2$
(i) $CuCO_3 \rightarrow CuO + CO_2$

Exercise 1.16 Equations (iii)

1. (a) $C + O_2 \rightarrow CO_2$
   (b) $2P + 3Cl_2 \rightarrow 2PCl_3$
   (c) $C + 2Br_2 \rightarrow CBr_4$
   (d) $C_4H_8 + 6O_2 \rightarrow 4CO_2 + 4H_2O$
   (e) $2H_2O_2 \rightarrow 2H_2O + O_2$

2. (a) $2CO + O_2 \rightarrow 2CO_2$
   (b) $H_2 + Cl_2 \rightarrow 2HCl$
   (c) $CH_4 + 2O_2 \rightarrow CO_2 + 2H_2O$
   (d) $2SO_2 + O_2 \rightarrow 2SO_3$
   (e) $2P + 3Cl_2 \rightarrow 2PCl_3$

3. (a) $2Mg(s) + O_2(g) \rightarrow 2MgO(s)$
   (b) $Mg(s) + 2AgNO_3(aq) \rightarrow Mg(NO_3)_2(aq) + 2Ag(s)$
   (c) $2NaOH(aq) + H_2SO_4(aq) \rightarrow Na_2SO_4(aq + 2H_2O(l)$
   (d) $2AgNO_3(aq) + BaCl_2(aq) \rightarrow Ba(NO_3)_2(aq) + 2AgCl(s)$
   (e) $2Na(s) + 2H_2O(l) \rightarrow 2NaOH(aq) + H_2(g)$
   (f) $2Al(s) + 3Cl_2(g) \rightarrow 2AlCl_3(s)$

4. (a) $4Na + O_2 \rightarrow 2Na_2O$
   (b) $2Mg + SO_2 \rightarrow 2MgO + S$
   (c) $Ca + H_2SO_4 \rightarrow CaSO_4 + H_2$
   (d) $CaO + H_2SO_4 \rightarrow CaSO_4 + H_2O$
   (e) $K_2CO_3 + 2HCl \rightarrow 2KCl + CO_2 + H_2O$
   (f) $K_2SO_4 + Ba(NO_3)_2 \rightarrow 2KNO_3 + BaSO_4$

5. (a) $2SO_2 + O_2 \rightarrow 2SO_3$
   (b) $Mg + F_2 \rightarrow MgF_2$
   (c) $C + 2Cl_2 \rightarrow CCl_4$
   (d) $C_3H_8 + 5O_2 \rightarrow 3CO_2 + 4H_2O$
   (e) $4Al + 3O_2 \rightarrow 2Al_2O_3$
   (f) $4NH_3 + 3O_2 \rightarrow 2N_2 + 6H_2O$
   (g) $2C_2H_2 + 5O_2 \rightarrow 4CO_2 + 2H_2O$
   (h) $CuO + H_2 \rightarrow Cu + H_2O$

6. (a) $2NaOH(aq) + H_2SO_4(aq) \rightarrow Na_2SO_4(aq) + 2H_2O(l)$
   (b) $MgO(s) + 2HNO_3(aq) \rightarrow Mg(NO_3)_2(aq) + H_2O(l)$
   (c) $K_2CO_3(aq) + 2HCl(aq) \rightarrow 2KCl(aq) + CO_2(g) + H_2O(l)$
   (d) $2Al(s) + 3H_2SO_4(aq) \rightarrow Al_2(SO_4)_3(aq) + 3H_2(g)$

6. (a) $AgNO_3(aq) + NaCl(aq) \rightarrow AgCl(s) + NaNO_3(aq)$
(b) $2NaOH(aq) + PbCl_2(aq) \rightarrow Pb(OH)_2(s) + 2NaCl(aq)$
(c) $BaCl_2(aq) + Na_2SO_4(aq) \rightarrow BaSO_4(s) + 2NaCl(aq)$
(d) $Ca(NO_3)_2(aq) + K_2CO_3(aq) \rightarrow 2KNO_3(aq) + CaCO_3(s)$
(e) $2FeCl_3(aq) + 3Ba(OH)_2(aq) \rightarrow 2Fe(OH)_3(s) + 3BaCl_2(aq)$

7. (1) $Ge + 2Cl_2 \rightarrow GeCl_4$
(2) $GeCl_4 + 2H_2O \rightarrow GeO_2 + 4HCl$
(3) $GeO_2 + 2H_2 \rightarrow Ge + 2H_2O$

> Note that in Step 2, "germanium oxide" should be "germanium chloride".

8. $\mathbf{X}_2 + 2\mathbf{Y}_2 \rightarrow 2\mathbf{XY}_2$

Exercise 1.17 — The mole

1. (a) 18 (b) 16 (c) 100 (d) 142
(e) 148.5 (f) 17 (g) 44 (h) 138
(i) 102 (j) 53.5

2. (a) 42 g (b) 40.5 g (c) 138 g (d) 180 g
(e) 132 g (f) 95.5 g (g) 56 g (h) 56 g
(i) 120.5 g (j) 85 g

3. (a) 46 g (b) 13.6 g (c) 37.125 g
(d) 320 g (e) 8.1 g (f) 48 g

> Note: (c) Formula should be $Mg(NO_3)_2$

4. (a) 3 mol (b) 0.2 mol (c) 0.1 mol
(d) 0.0187 mol (e) 0.05 mol (f) 49.58 mol

5. 0.015 mol

6. 25 mol

7. 0.00499 mol

8. (a)

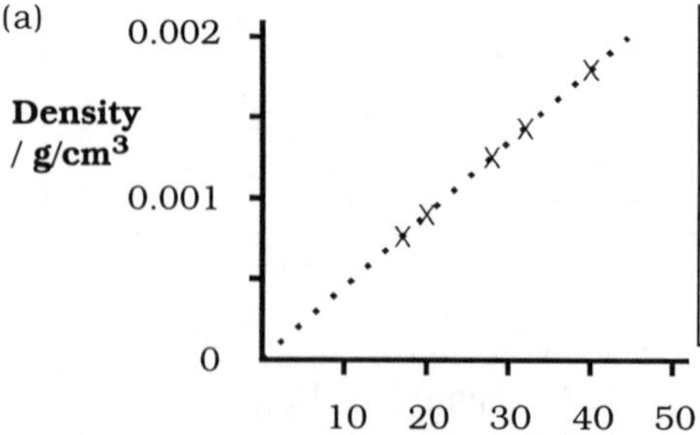

> Note: Densities are only provided for elements in the data booklet.
> Relevant densities (in g / cm^3) for compounds are:
> ammonia 0.0076
> carbon monoxide 0.00125
> ethane 0.00893

(b) (i) 34 (ii) CH_3F

9. (a) 2 mol l^{-1} (b) 2g

Exercise 1.18 Using balanced equations

1. 4.68 g
2. 8.8 g
3. 3.1 g
4. 12 g
5. 2.4 g
6. 3.16 g
7. $4,36 \times 10^5$ kg
8. 660 kg
9. 10 g
10. 906.3 tonnes
11. 4200 kg
12. 38.8 g
13. 176 tonnes

Unit 2

Exercise 2.1 Fuels

1. A fuel is a substance which can be burned to release energy.
   Combustion is a chemical reaction in which a substance combines with oxygen to release energy.

2. Take a sample of each gas and test it with a burning splint; the one which relights the splint is oxygen.
   Take a fresh sample of the remaining gases and test each with limewater; the one which turns limewater milky is carbon dioxide.
   The remaining gas is nitrogen by elimination.

3. (a) hydrocarbons
   (b) (i) Separation of a mixture of substances in a liquid, according to the boiling point, by raising the temperature to evaporate individual substances from the mixture at different temperatures and condensing them back into the liquid state.
   (ii) A component of a mixture of liquids which has a fixed range of boiling points.
   (c) (i) fuel for cars (ii) fuel for lorries (iii) fuel for camping stoves
   (iv) fuel for jet aircraft (v) making tar for roads

4. (a) (i) A substance which can catch fire easily.
   (ii) A liquid which can flow only slowly.
   (b) (i) gas (ii) bitumen

5. (a) nitrogen and oxygen
   (b) The spark from the spark plug provides sufficient energy to allow nitrogen and oxygen to combine.

6. (a) It is a poisonous gas (dissolves in water forming acid rain).
   (b) It is cheaper to obtain.

7. (a) exothermic
   (b) oxygen
   (c) carbon dioxide, water
   (d) In an insufficient supply of air, paraffin will burn to produce some carbon monoxide which is poisonous.

8. (a) The supply of air to the burning fuel is limited and combustion will be incomplete.
   (b) sulphur dioxide
   (c) Industries use large quantities of energy which is produced mainly by the combustion of fossil fuels. These contain impurities which burn to contribute to atmospheric pollution.
   (d) For example, the use of catalytic converters in cars.

9. (a) sulphur, carbon, hydrogen
   (b) fractional distillation

10. (a) oxygen
    (b) It is made up of very small particles with a large surface area and will react very quickly with oxygen.
    (c) carbon monoxide

11. (a) carbon, hydrogen, oxygen
    (b) A compound which contains carbon and hydrogen only.

12. (a) North Sea crude oil contains a higher proportion of petroleum spirit and gasolines for which demand is very heavy as fuel for cars.
    (b) fractional distillation

13. (a) (i) gas (ii) petrol (iii) kerosine (iv) diesel (v) bitumen
    (b) (i) petrol (ii) smaller, lighter molecules, therefore more easily evaporated

14. (a) Less sulphur dioxide is being released into the atmosphere each year.
    (b) Removal of sulphur dioxide from waste gases of power stations, or reduction in the use of coal and oil fired power stations.
    (c) (i) oxides of nitrogen, carbon monoxide
        (ii) Sparking of air in car engines allows nitrogen and oxygen to combine. Incomplete combustion of fuel allows the formation of carbon monoxide.

15. (a) The mixture contains enough oxygen for the complete combustion of the fuel to give carbon dioxide.
    (b) nitrogen oxides
    (c) It reduces the concentration of oxides of nitrogen in the exhaust by a significant amount.

16. (a) (i) Combination of oxygen and nitrogen from the air because of the energy supplied by the spark plug.
        (ii) Limited supply of oxygen in the car engine giving incomplete combustion of the hydrocarbons in the fuel.
    (b) nitrogen, carbon dioxide

17. (a) (b) 88%

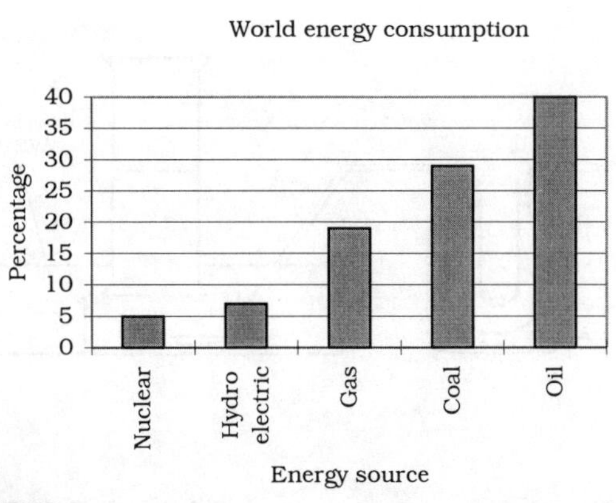

18. (a) **E**

(b **A** - carbon dioxide is denser than air and there would be too much mixing of air and carbon dioxide.

B - carbon dioxide would not collect in the gas jar because it is denser than air.

C - carbon dioxide is fairly soluble in water.

D - carbon dioxide is entering a closed system and cannot displace air.

19.

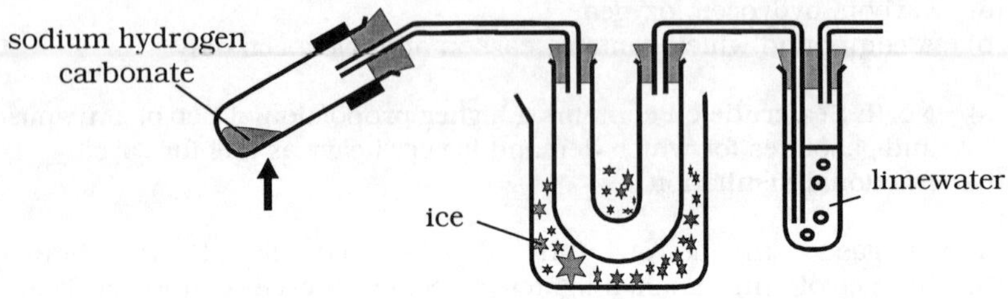

20.

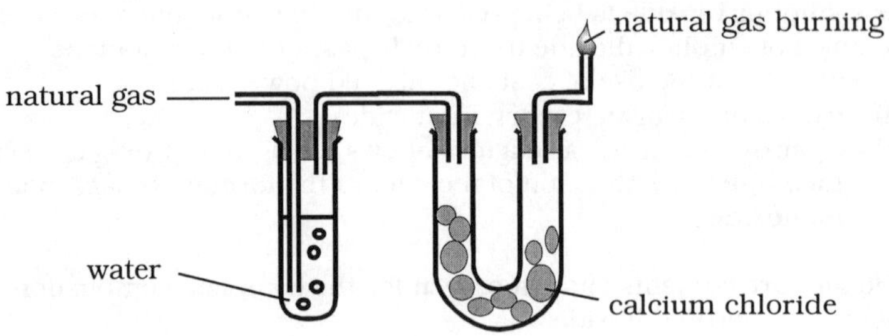

21. (a) They must contain some hydrogen.

(b) To ensure that the concentration of green colour to estimate the quantity of sulphur dioxide released can be compared.

(c) To measure the flow rate of the oxygen to ensure that comparisons are fair.

22. (a) To prevent combustion of the plastic.

(b)

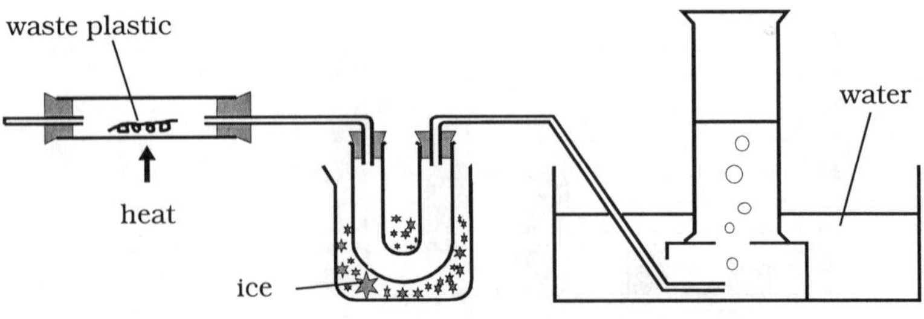

23. (a) carbon dioxide, water

(b)

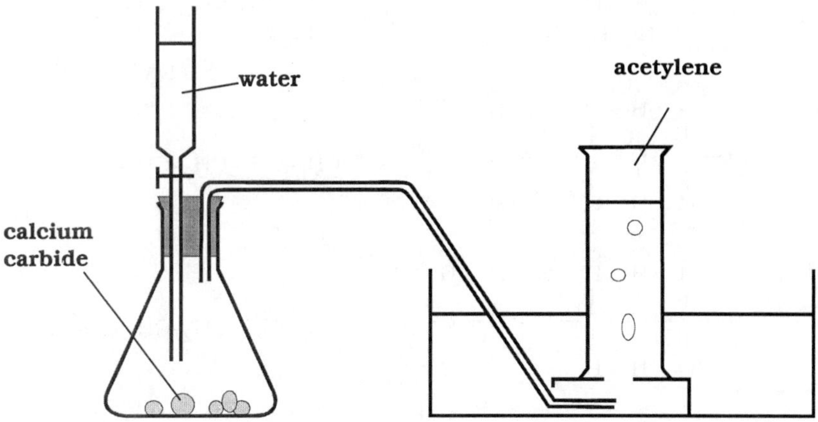

Exercise 2.2 Nomenclature and structure - hydrocarbons

1. (a) hexane (b) propene (c) cyclobutane
   (d) pent-2-ene (e) pentane (f) but-2-ene
   (g) cyclohexane

2. (a)

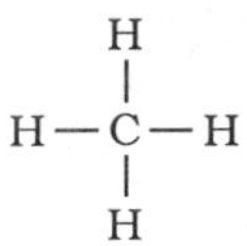

CH_4

(b)

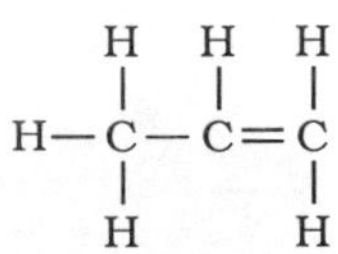

$CH_3–CH=CH_2$

(c)

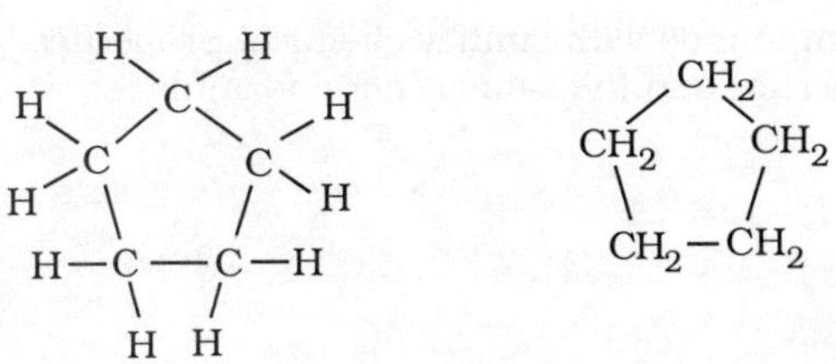

(d) 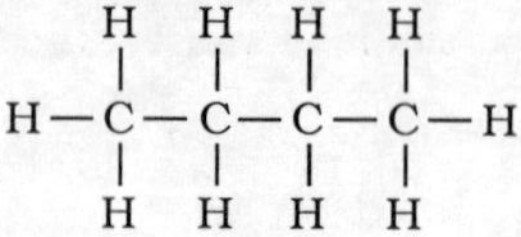

$CH_3–CH_2–CH_2–CH_3$

(e) 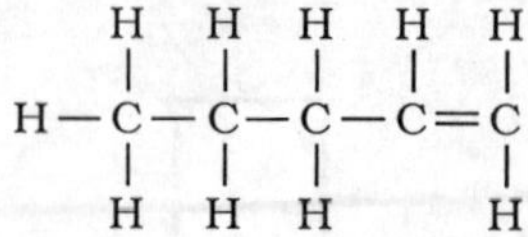

$CH_3–CH_2–CH_2–CH=CH_2$

(f) 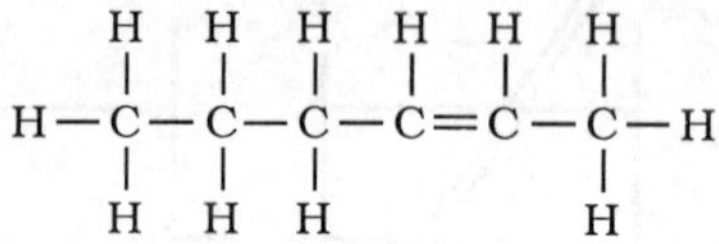

$CH_3–CH_2–CH_2–CH=CH–CH_3$

3. (a) 2-methylpentane (b) 2,3-dimethylbutane
(c) 3-methylpentane (d) 2,2-dimethylbutane

4. (a) 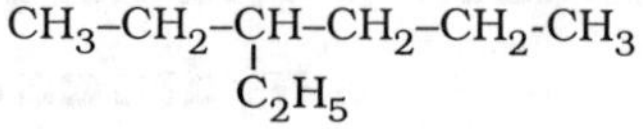

(b) 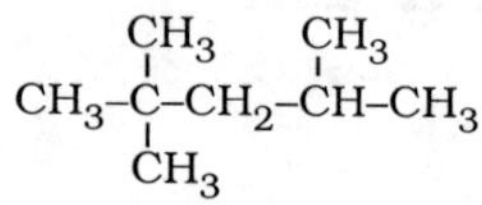

(c) 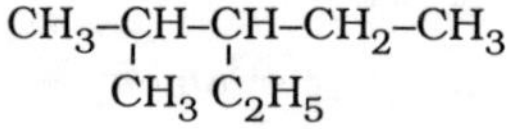

(d) $CH_2=CH–CH=CH–CH_3$

5. (a) C_8H_{18} (b) C_6H_{12} (c) C_6H_{12}
(d) $C_{12}H_{26}$ (e) $C_{10}H_{20}$ (f) C_8H_{16}

6. (a) C_nH_{2n-2}
(b) 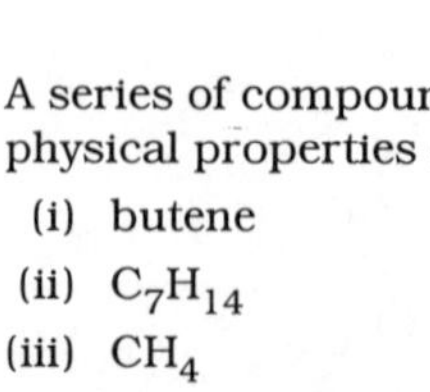

7. (a) A series of compounds with similar chemical properties, gradually changing physical properties and the same general formula.
(b) (i) butene
(ii) C_7H_{14}
(iii) CH_4

8. $C_nH_{2n+1}CHO$

9. (a) As the number of chlorine atoms in the molecule increases, the anaesthetic effect increases.

(b)

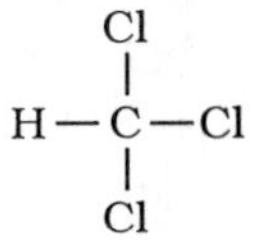

10. (a) Boiling points of alkanes

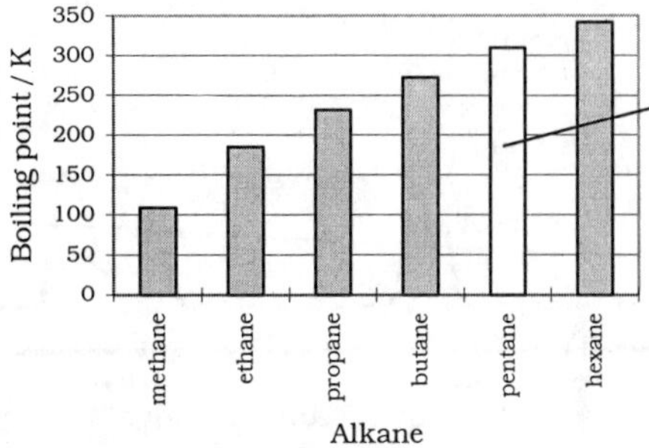

(b) b. pt. 310 K

(c) butane, pentane, hexane

11. Formula mass against number of carbon atoms.

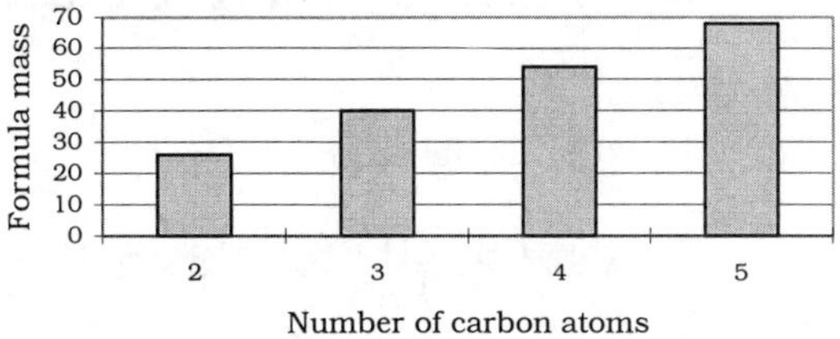

(b) 82

(c) C_2H_2

12. (a) Cracking of naphtha

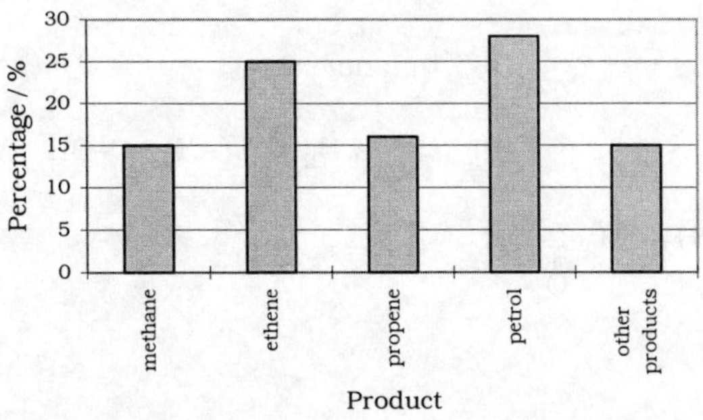

(b) alkenes

13. (a) hexane
    (b) shorter hydrocarbon chain, greater number of branches on the chain

14. (a) The greater the number of carbon atoms, the longer the time taken to pass through the column.

    Isomers of the same alkane which contain more branches pass through the column more quickly.

    (b)

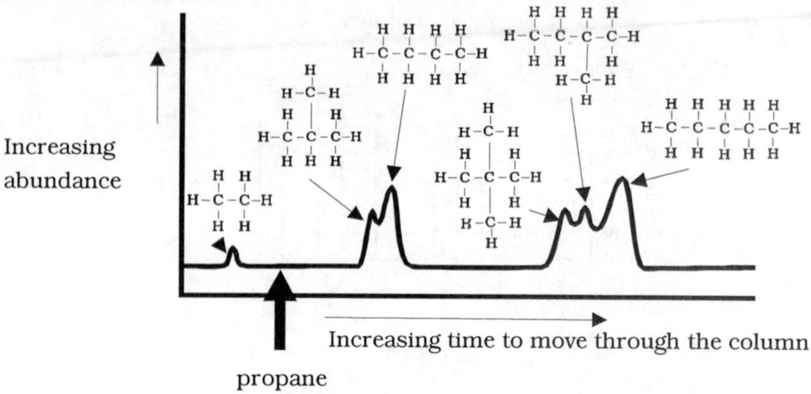

Exercise 2.3 Nomenclature and structure - alkanols and alkanoic acids

1. (a) ethanol (b) butan-2-ol
   (c) propan-1-ol (d) pentan-2-ol

2. (a) CH_3-OH (b) $CH_3-\underset{\displaystyle OH}{\underset{|}{CH}}-CH_2-CH_2-CH_2-CH_3$

   (c) $CH_3-CH_2-\underset{\displaystyle OH}{\underset{|}{CH}}-CH_2-CH_3$ (d) $CH_3-CH_2-\overset{\displaystyle CH_3}{\overset{|}{\underset{\displaystyle CH_3}{\underset{|}{C}}}}-CH_2-OH$

3. (a) methanoic acid (b) butanoic acid

4. (a) $CH_3-\underset{\displaystyle O}{\underset{\|}{C}}-OH$ (b) $CH_3-CH_2-CH_2-CH_2-\underset{\displaystyle O}{\underset{\|}{C}}-OH$

   (c) $CH_3-CH_2-CH_2-CH_2-CH_2-\underset{\displaystyle O}{\underset{\|}{C}}-OH$

Exercise 2.4 Nomenclature and structure - esters

1. (a) methyl ethanoate (b) methyl methanoate
   (c) propyl ethanoate (d) ethyl methanoate

2. (a) $CH_3 - \underset{\underset{O}{\|}}{C} - O - CH_2 - CH_3$

   (b) $CH_3 - CH_2 - CH_2 - \underset{\underset{O}{\|}}{C} - O - CH_2 - CH_2 - CH_3$

3. (a) ethyl methanoate $H - \underset{\underset{O}{\|}}{C} - O - CH_2 - CH_3$

   (b) methyl propanoate $CH_3 - CH_2 - \underset{\underset{O}{\|}}{C} - O - CH_3$

   (c) ethyl ethanoate $CH_3 - \underset{\underset{O}{\|}}{C} - O - CH_2 - CH_3$

   (d) propyl methanoate $H - \underset{\underset{O}{\|}}{C} - O - CH_2 - CH_2 - CH_3$

4. (a) ethanol

   $CH_3 - CH_2 - OH$

   propanoic acid

   $CH_3 - CH_2 - \underset{\underset{O}{\|}}{C} - OH$

   (b) methanol

   $CH_3 - OH$

   ethanoic acid

   $CH_3 - \underset{\underset{O}{\|}}{C} - OH$

   (c) ethanol

   $CH_3 - CH_2 - OH$

   methanoic acid

   $H - \underset{\underset{O}{\|}}{C} - OH$

   (d) methanol

   $CH_3 - OH$

   butanoic acid

   $CH_3 - CH_2 - CH_2 - \underset{\underset{O}{\|}}{C} - OH$

Exercise 2.5 Isomers

1. (a) **B** (b) **B** (c) **B** (d) **B** (e) **B** (f) **A**
   (g) **A** (h) **B** (i) **B** (j) **A** (k) **B** (l) **A**

2. (a) $CH_3\text{–}CH_2\text{–}CH_2\text{–}CH_2\text{–}CH_3$ pentane

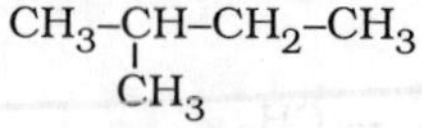

methylbutane

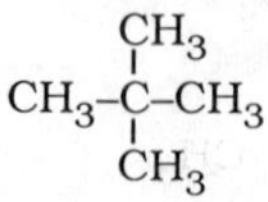

dimethylpropane

   (b) $CH_2{=}CH\text{–}CH_2\text{–}CH_2\text{–}CH_2\text{–}CH_3$ hex-1-ene
   $CH_3\text{–}CH{=}CH\text{–}CH_2\text{–}CH_2\text{–}CH_3$ hex-2-ene
   $CH_3\text{–}CH_2\text{–}CH{=}CH\text{–}CH_2\text{–}CH_3$ hex-3-ene

3. $CH_3\text{–}CH_2\text{–}CH_2\text{–}CH_2\text{–}OH$

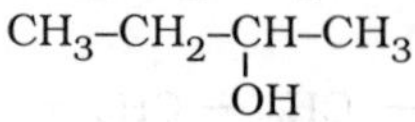

4. 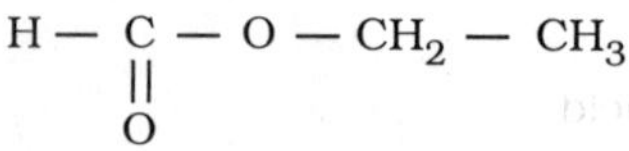

ethyl methanoate

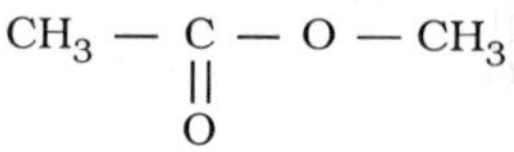

methyl ethanoate

Exercise 2.6 Reactions of carbon compounds

1. (a) (i) A compound of carbon and hydrogen in which all the carbon to carbon bonds are single bonds.
   (ii) A compound of carbon and hydrogen containing at least one carbon to carbon double bond.
   (b) (i) butane, octane, methane (ii) ethene, butene

2. (a) 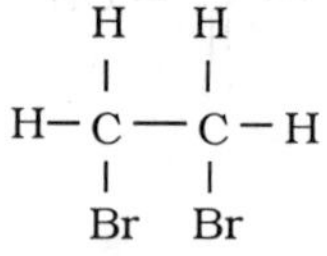
   (b) addition (c) ethane

3. (a) unsaturated (b) addition (c) 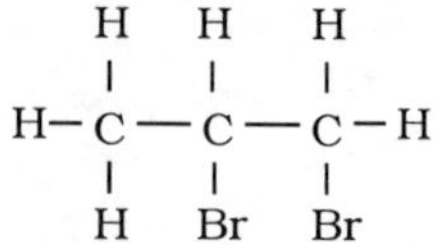

4. Shake with bromine solution. The bromine will decolourise rapidly in the absence of light.

5. $C_4H_6Br_2$ $C_6H_{10}Br_2$

6.

A - hexene

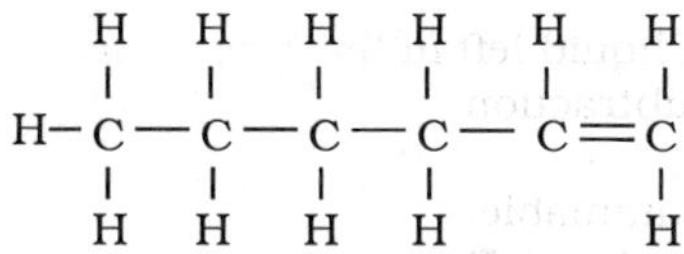

B - hexane

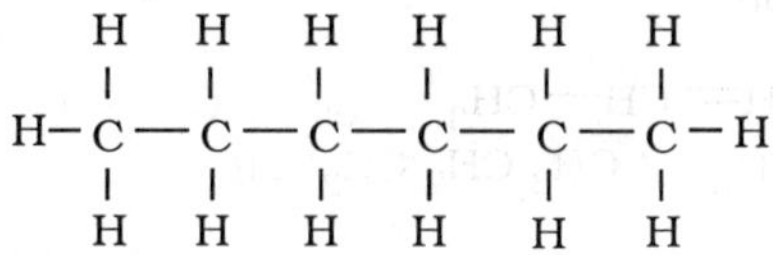

C - cyclohexane

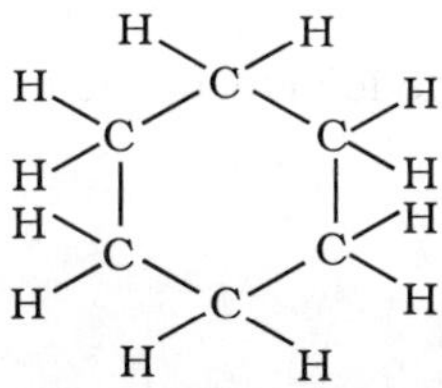

7. (a) A compound of carbon and hydrogen containing at least one double bond.

(b)

$C_{10}H_{16}Br_4$,

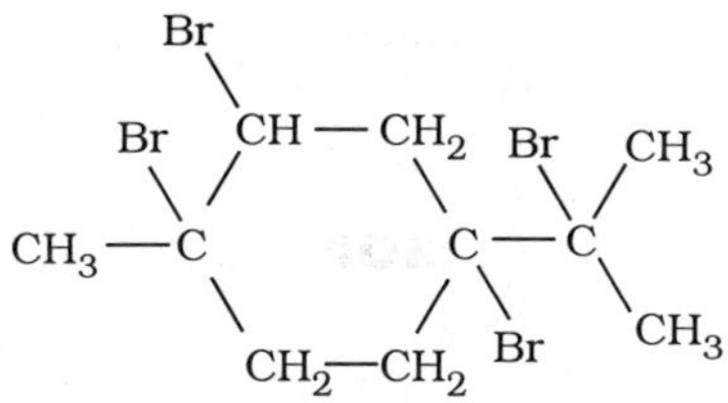

8. (a)

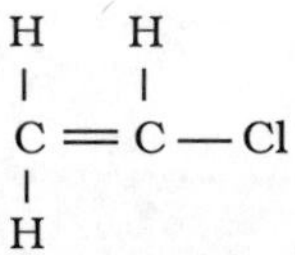

(b) hydrogen chloride

9. (a) (i)

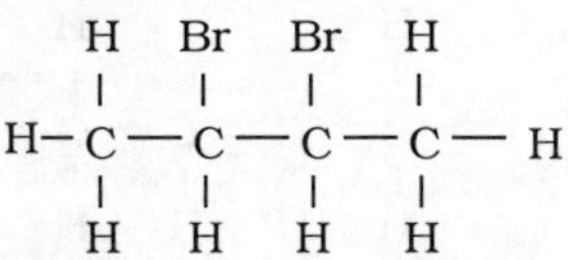

(ii)

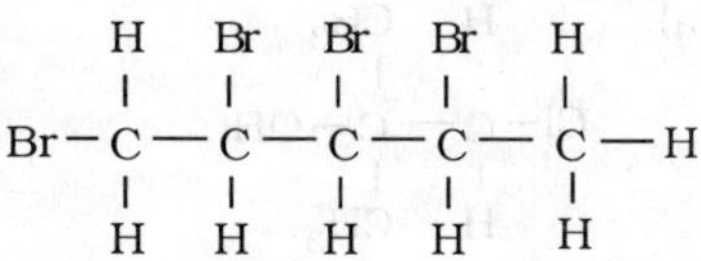

(b) addition

10. Measure 10 cm^3 of oil into the beaker using the measuring cylinder.

Fill the syringe carefully with iodine solution and note the volume of solution in the syringe.

Add iodine solution dropwise to the beaker, stirring, until one drop of iodine solution retains its colour.

Note the volume of liquid left in the syringe and find the volume of iodine solution used by subtraction.

11. (a) They are all flammable.
(b) Add sodium to **A** and **B**; only **A** will give off a gas.
(c) no reaction

12. (a) $CH_3—CH=CH—CH_3$ or $CH_2=CH—CH_2—CH_3$
(b) 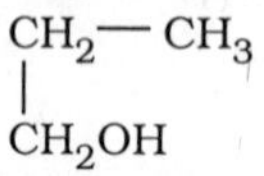 ($CH_3\ CH_2\ CH_2OH$)

13. (a) butane (b) iodomethane, iodoethane
(c) 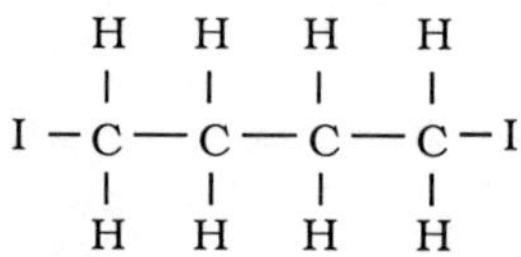

14. (a) 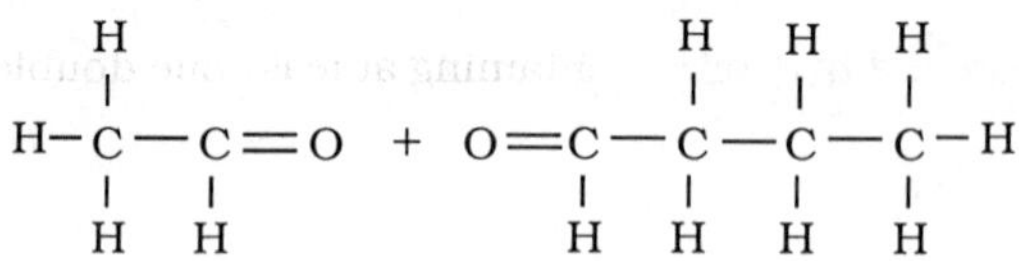

(b) 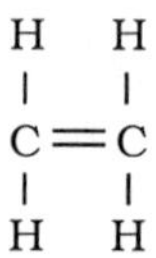

15. (a) 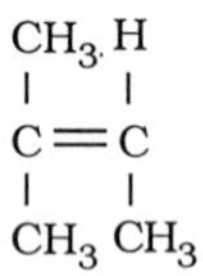 (b) 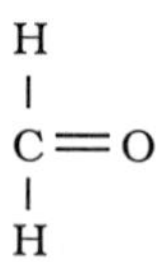

16. (a) 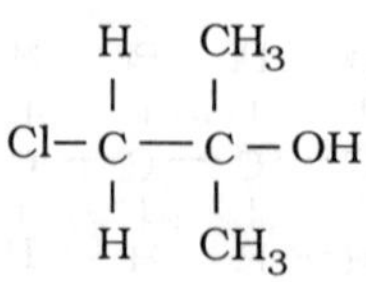 (b) 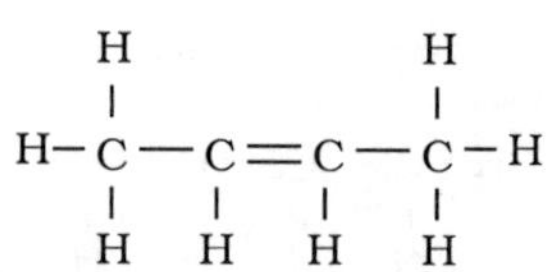

Exercise 2.7 Cracking

1. (a) Breaking down a long chain alkane to give a shorter chain alkane and an alkene.

   (b)

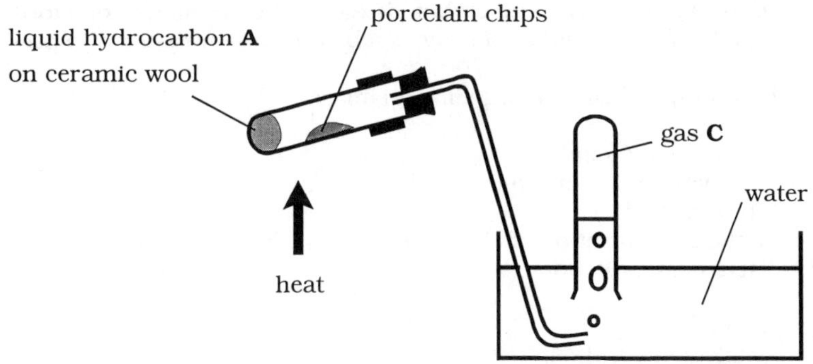

   (c) e.g. steel wool, porcelain, aluminium oxide, or aluminium silicate

   (d) **A** - octane, **B** - hexane

   (e) C_2H_4, ethene

   (f) Shake **A** and **C** with bromine solution.
   A will only decolourise bromine solution slowly in the presence of light;
   C will decolourise bromine solution quickly in the absence of light.

   (g) It converts fractions for which supply is greater than demand into fractions for which demand is greater than supply.

2. (a) It is saturated.

   (b) (i) It is unsaturated. (ii) cracking

   (iii) Lift the apparatus clear of the heat and water to avoid "sucking back".

3. (a) It would reduce the amount of heat energy required.

   (b) There are insufficient hydrogen atoms to produce two alkane molecules as products therefore a (saturated) alkane and an (unsaturated) alkene are produced.

4. (a) The chain length will be shorter.
   One molecule will contain a double bond.

   (b) More gas oil is produced than can be sold, but the supply of gasoline is much smaller than market demand. Gas oil is therefore cracked to meet this demand.

Exercise 2.8 Ethanol

1. (a) fermentation
   (b) a suitable plant source, eg grapes, barley, sugar cane, etc.
   (c) The juice of grapes is treated with yeast. The glucose is fermented by the yeast to give alcohol and carbon dioxide. When fermentation stops, the liquid is filtered and the filtrate can be fractionally distilled to produce alcohol.
   (d) for example, heart damage, liver damage

2. (a) (i) carbon dioxide
   (ii) zymase, an enzyme
   (iii) ethanol
   (b) As the concentration of ethanol increases, the yeast dies.
   (c) fractional distillation

3. (a) ethene
   (b) (catalytic) hydration

4. (a) dehydration
   (b) $CH_3–CH=CH_2$

Exercise 2.9 Making and breaking esters

1. (a) ethanol, butan-2-ol
   (b) The reaction is reversible and eventually reaches equilibrium.

2. (a) condensation
   (b) **X** unused ethanol, unused ethanoic acid
   Y ethyl ethanoate

3.

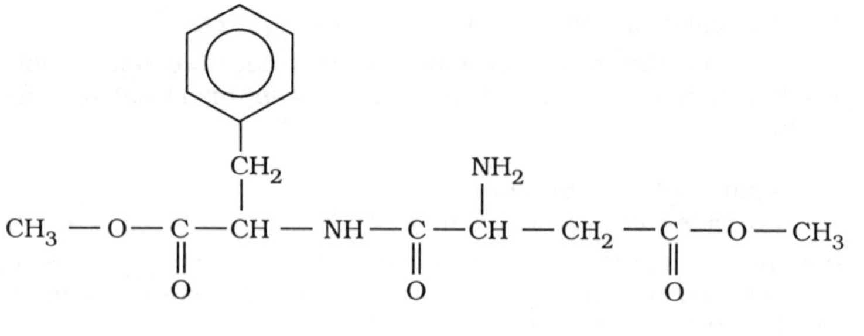

4. (a)

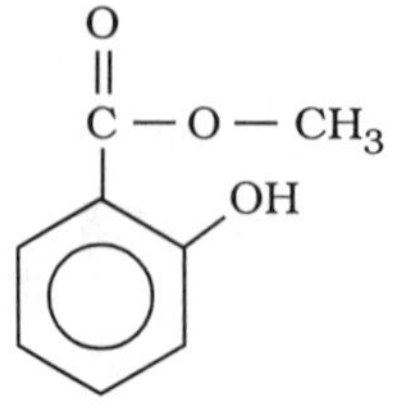

(b) (i) Breaking down a molecule into two or more smaller molecules by the action of water.

(ii) 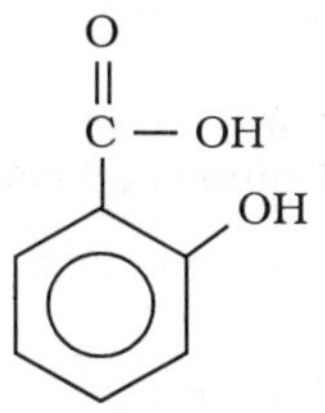 and $CH_3-\underset{\underset{\displaystyle O}{||}}{C}-OH$

(iii) Hydrolysis of aspirin by heat and moisture forms ethanoic acid which smells of vinegar.

5. (a) $CH_3-\underset{\underset{\displaystyle O}{||}}{C}-OH$

(b) hydrolysis

Exercise 2.10 Plastics and synthetic fibres

1. (a) A natural material can be used without being chemically changed. A synthetic material is man-made.
   (b) crude oil
   (c) for example, terylene, nylon

2. (a)

Plastic	Uses
polythene	washing-up bowls, waste-bin liners
polyvinyl chloride	window frames, pipes, guttering
melamine	plates, tumblers
perspex	safety screens, spectacle lenses
bakelite	electric plugs and switches
polystyrene	packaging, ceiling tiles

(b) polythene - easily moulded
polyvinyl chloride - resistant to chemical attack
melamine - does not soften on heating
perspex - strong, does not shatter like glass
bakelite - good electrical insulator
polystyrene - good heat insulator, light weight

3. (a) light weight, very resistant to chemical attack
   (b) (i) poisonous gases
   (ii) not biodegradable

4. (a) non-stick
   (b) waterproof
   (c) good electrical insulator

5. (a) (i) A plastic which does not soften on heating.
   (ii) A plastic which softens and melts on heating and can then be moulded.
   (b) (i) thermosetting
   (ii) thermoplastic

6. (a) It will not decompose when acted upon by bacteria.
   (b) thermoplastic

7. (a) A plastic which can be broken down by the action of bacteria.
   (b) (i) They are very durable in uses where they are exposed to weather and soil.
   (ii) They are difficult to dispose of and create a litter problem for many years.

8. Kevlar very strong
   poly(ethenol) water soluble
   Biopol biodegradable

9. (a) **A, B** and **C** (b) **C** (c) **A**

Exercise 2.11 Making polymers (i)

1. (a) (i) Monomers are small molecules which can join together to form very large molecules (polymers).
   (ii) A very large molecule made by joining together many small molecules.
   (b) polymerisation
   (c) (i) polystyrene (ii) poly(propene) (iii) polyvinyl chloride
   (d) All have a carbon to carbon double bond.
   (e) (i) crude oil
   (ii) fractional distillation and cracking.

2. a) (i) ethene
   (ii)

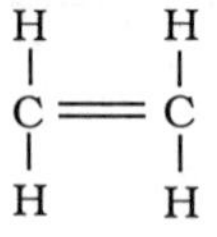

   (b)

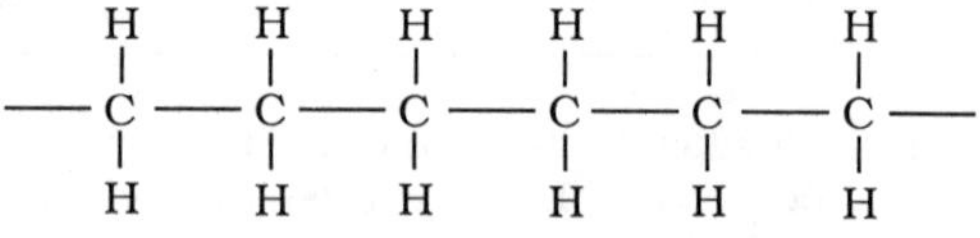

3. (a) A very large molecule made by a large number of monomer units joining together by the opening of carbon to carbon double bonds with no other products being formed.
   (b) 3
   (c)

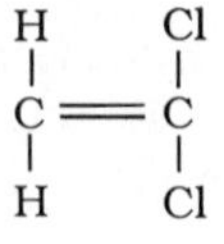

4. (a) (i) propene

(ii) 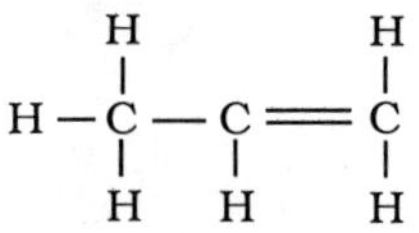

(b) 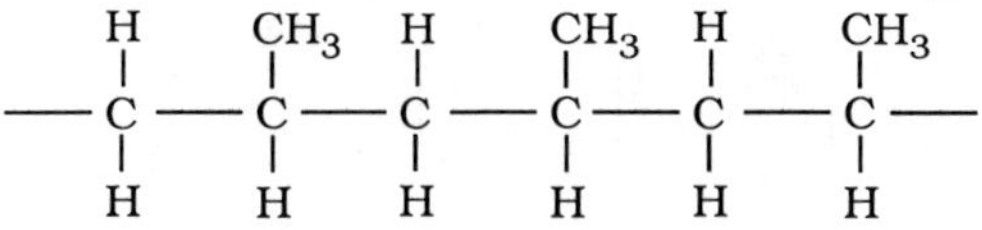

5. (a) 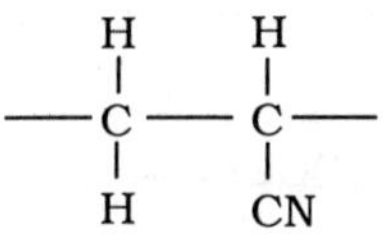

(b) 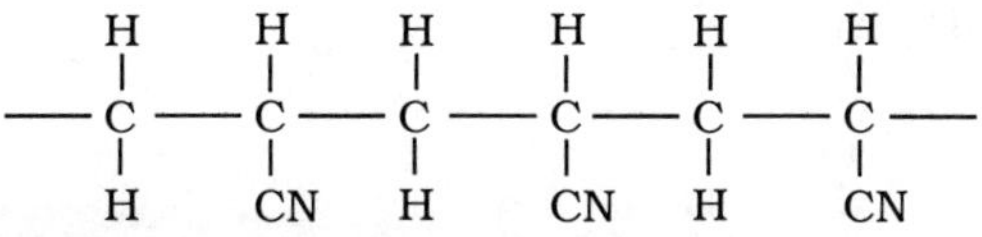

6. (a) 4

(b) 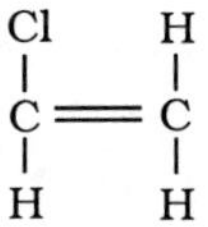

(c) addition

7. (a) poly(tetrafluoroethene)

(b) 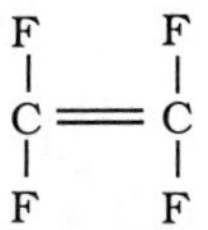

(c) 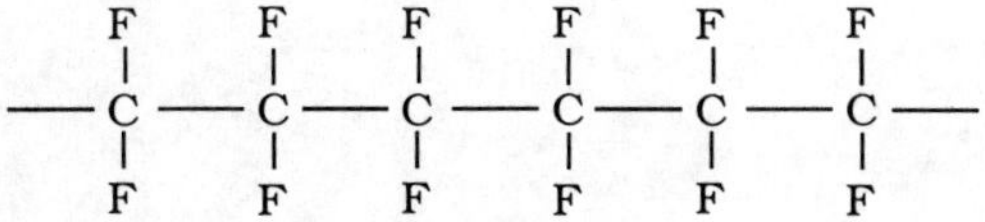

8. (a) Add bromine solution to each. Phenylethene will rapidly decolourise the bromine solution.
(b) phenylethene
(c) addition
(d)

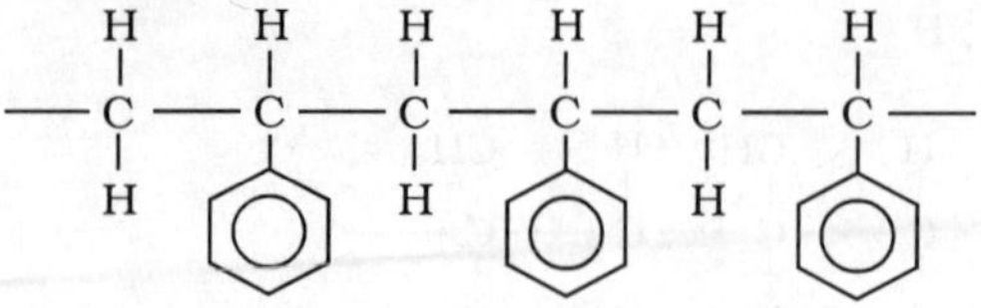

9. (a)

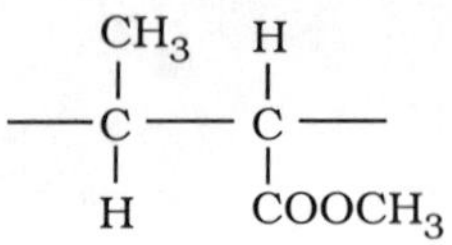

(b)

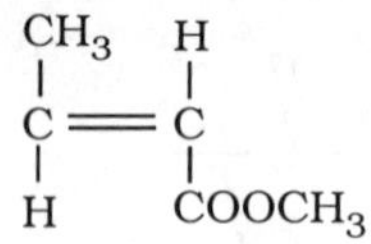

10. (a)

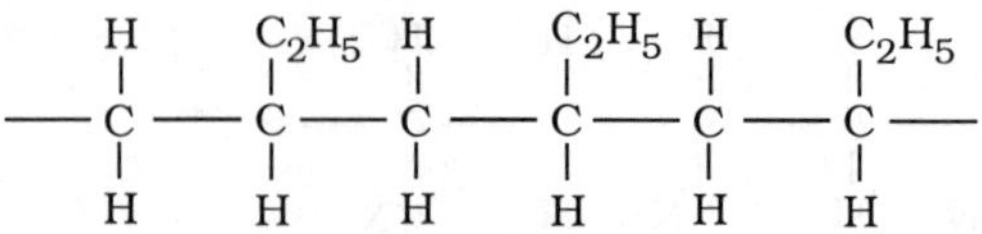

(b) (i)

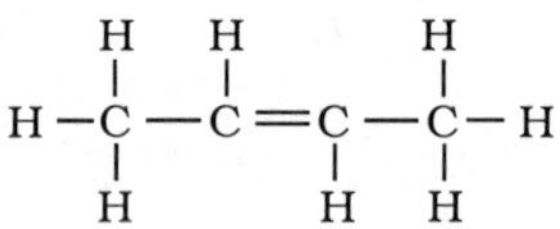

(ii)

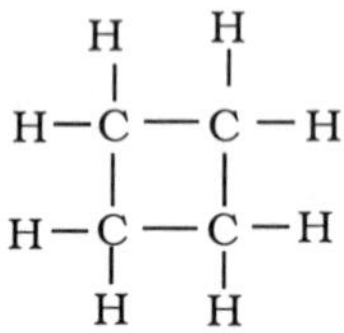

11. a)

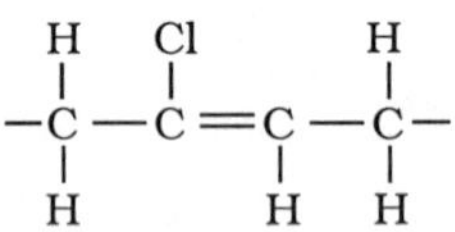

(b) The polymer will decolourise bromine solution quickly.

12. (a) addition
(b)

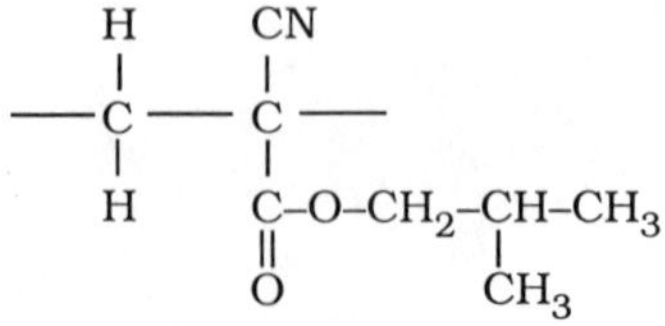

Note: Original question should be numbered 12.

Exercise 2.12 Making polymers (ii)

1. (a) water
   (b)

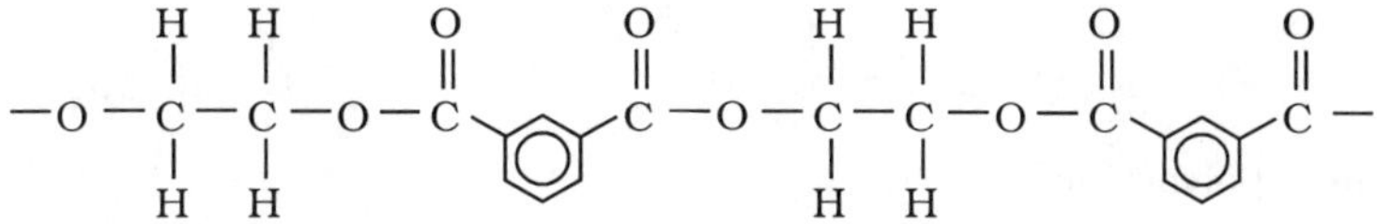

   (c) for example, nylon

2. (a) **A** - a diamine **B** - a dicarboxylic acid
   (b) condensation
   (c)

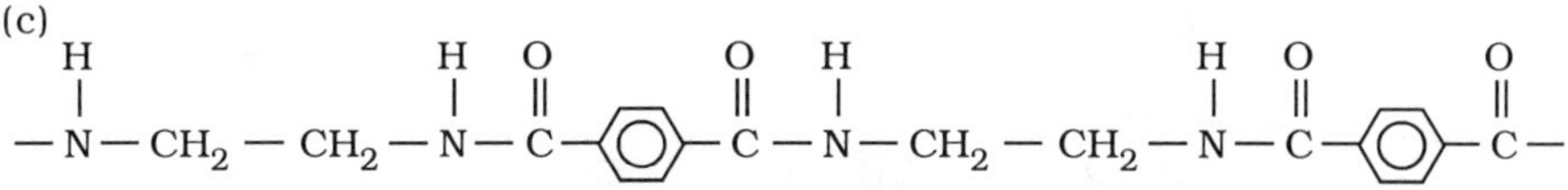

3. (a)

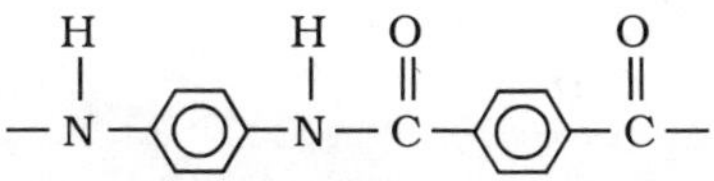

   (b)

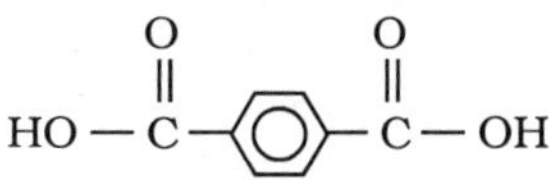

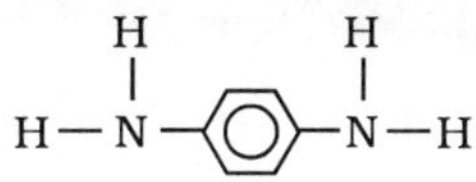

   (c) condensation

4. (a)

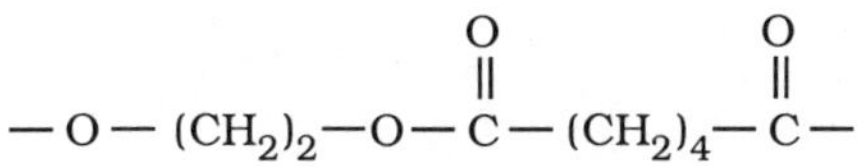

   (b)

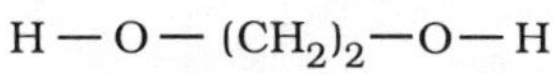

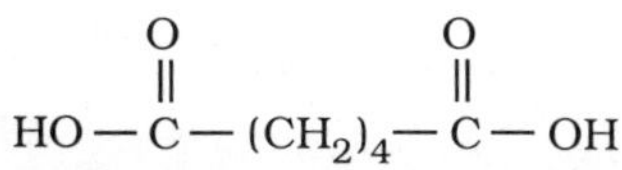

5. (a) (i)

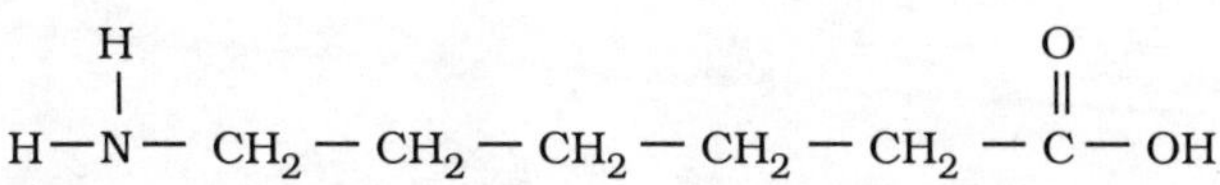

   (ii)

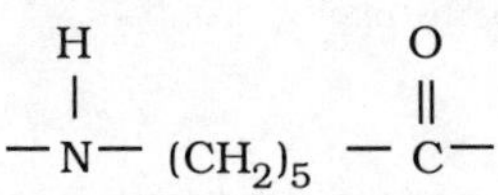

b) i) 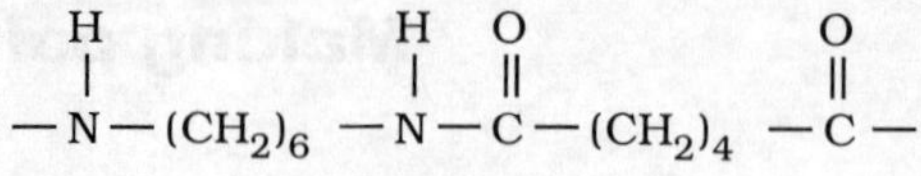

ii) 

iii) polyamide

6. 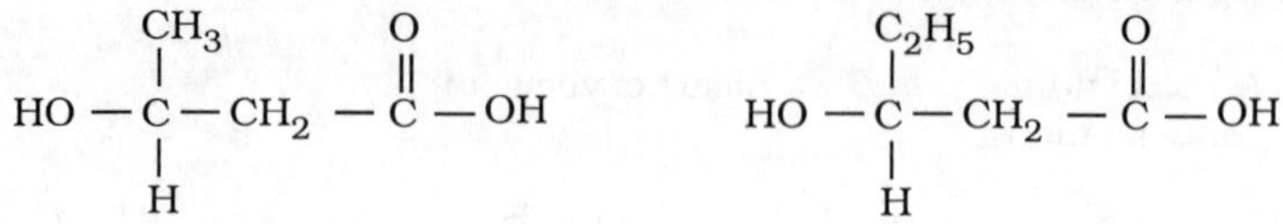

7. (a)

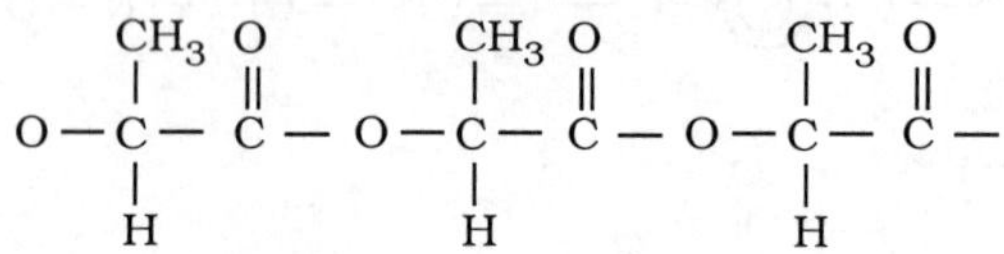

(b) condensation

Exercise 2.13 Carbohydrates

1. (a) carbon, hydrogen, oxygen
   (b) They combine with oxygen to provide the body with energy.

2. (a) sucrose
   (b) (i) starch (ii) glucose (iii) amylase, an enzyme

3. Test a little of all three solids with a drop of iodine solution. The solid which turns blue/black is starch.
   Dissolve the remaining two solids in water and add enough Benedict's solution to each to give a blue colour. Place in a beaker of boiling water. The solution which gives a brick red precipitate is glucose.

4. Glucose is soluble and can be absorbed directly through the gut wall into the bloodstream. Starch has to be broken down by enzymes in the digestive system to form glucose before it can be absorbed. This process is slower, so starch is unable to be used to supply energy as quickly.

5. (a) The breaking down of a large molecule into two or more smaller molecules by the action of water.
   (b) glucose
   (c) The glucose can be absorbed through the gut wall directly, but starch must be hydrolysed before absorption.

6. (a) No, it may be a hydrocarbon.
   (b) **X** is not starch.
   (c) **X** is not glucose, fructose or maltose.
   (d) (i) **X** is being broken down to form glucose, fructose or maltose.
       (ii) hydrolysis

7. (a) —O—[G]—O—[G]—O—[G]—
   (b) condensation

8. (a) sugars
   (b) an enzyme
   (c) Dissolve a little honey in water. Add Benedict's solution until a distinct blue colour can be seen. Place in a boiling water bath. A brick red precipitate indicates the presence of glucose.

9. (a) (i) no
       (ii) Becauses enzymes are destroyed by high temperature and can no longer catalyse hydrolysis at 100 °C.

10. (a) starch and iodine
    (b) the volume of solution **A**, the volume of solution **B**, the concentration of solution **B**, or temperature

Exercise 2.14 Proteins

1. (a) Proteins are essential for the growth and repair of tissue.
   (b) amino acids
   (c) carbon, hydrogen, oxygen and nitrogen

2. (a)

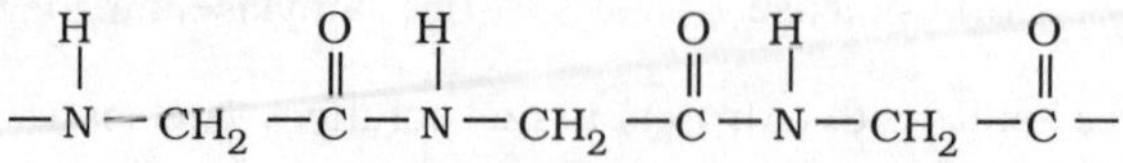

   (b) condensation polymerisation

3. (a)

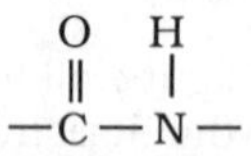

   (b) (i) 2
   (ii)

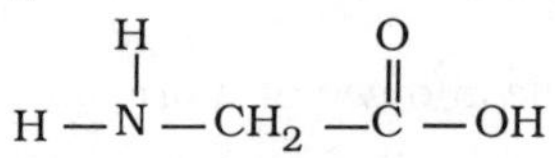

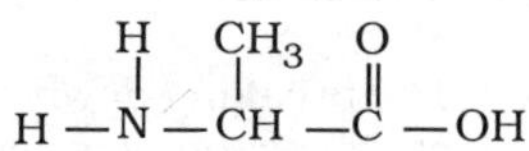

   (iii) hydrolysis

4. a)

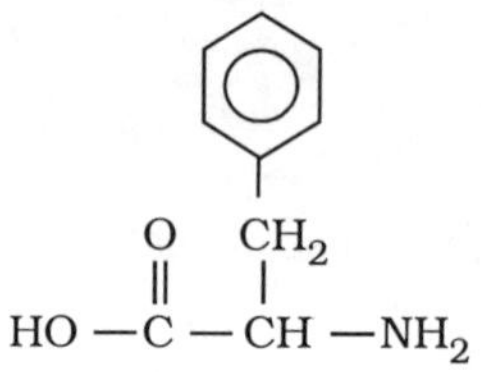

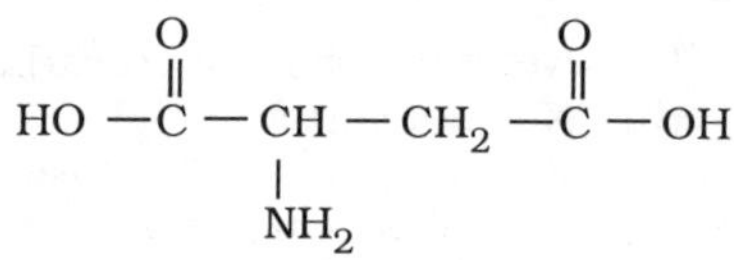

   b) Cooking would hydrolyse aspartame and its sweetness would be lost. In cold drinks, hydrolysis is very slow, an aspartame remains unchanged.

Exercise 2.15 Fats and oils

1. (a) They provide an efficient means by which the body can store energy.
   (b) The long saturated hydrocarbon chains in fats can twist into a relatively small volume, whereas the presence of the double bond in the hydrocarbon chains of an oil restricts this. The fat molecules are much more compact and larger van der Waals' forces can exist between fat molecules giving rise to melting points above room temperature. The smaller van der Waals' forces in oils give a lower melting point, below room temperature.

2. (a)

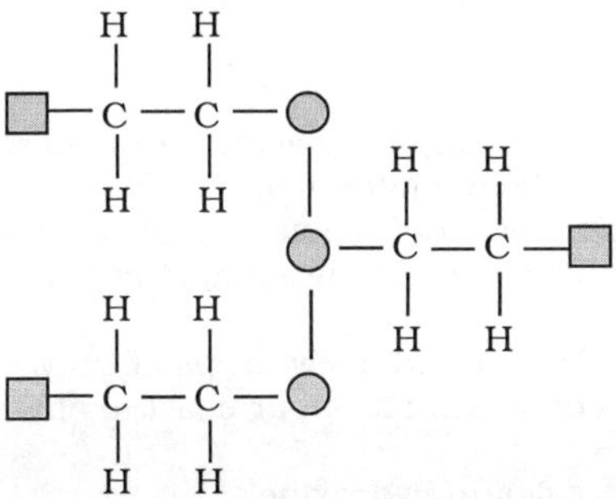

   (b) The melting point is increased.
   (c) (catalytic) hydrogenation

3. a)

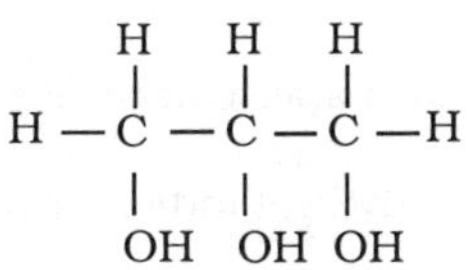

   b) 1:3

4. a) esters
   b)

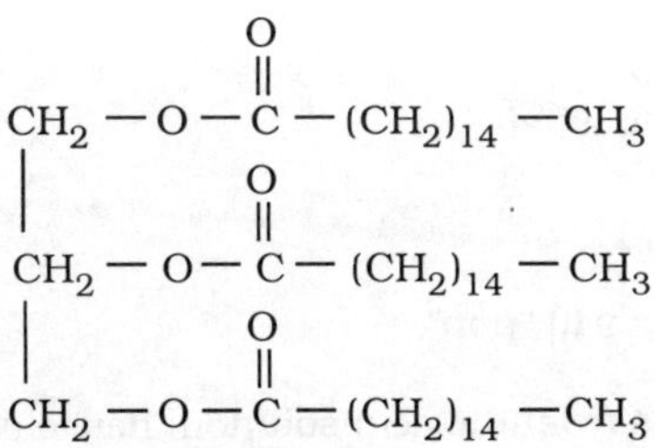

   c) It is likely to be a fat because the carbon chains are saturated.

5. a) (enzyme) hydrolysis
   b) i) saturated
      ii) glycerol (propan-1,2,3-triol)

Unit 3

Exercise 3.1 Acids and alkalis

1. (a) It is a measure of the acidity (or alkalinity) of a solution.
   (b) Add a drop of Universal indicator solution (or pH paper) and compare the colour with a colour chart to obtain the pH measurement.
   (c) yellow, orange, red
   (d) below 7
   (e) blue green, blue, purple
   (f) above 7
   (g) yellow green
   (h) 7

2. (a) (i) eg. nitric acid, sulphuric acid, hydrochloric acid
   (ii) eg. vinegar, lemon juice, cola
   (b) (i) eg. sodium hydroxide, potassium hydroxide, limewater
   (ii) eg. washing soda, baking soda, cleaners containing ammonia

3. (a) To a sample of water add a few drops of Universal indicator solution and compare the colour with a colour chart to obtain the pH value.
   (b) acid rain
   (c) any alkali, eg. calcium hydroxide

4. (a) broad beans, potatoes
   (b) lime

5. Citric acid must be dissolved in water before the pH paper can be used to measure the pH.
   The crystals can dissolve in the water present in Universal indicator solution, and will cause it to turn red.

6. (a) carbon dioxide, nitrogen dioxide
   (b) sodium hydroxide, calcium oxide

7. (a) A solution of the oxide of **A** is an acid.
   A solution of the oxide of **B** is an alkali.
   (b) Element **A** is a non-metal.
   Element **B** is a metal.

8. (a) Apply a lighted splint; hydrogen will "pop".
   (b) (i) negative
   (ii) It must attract $H^+(aq)$ ions from the acid solution, hence it must be negative.

9. (a) hydrogen ion
   (b) Water will dilute the acid and make it less corrosive.
   (c) The pH will increase (to a maximum value of 7).

10. (a) It increases
(b) The pH of the water will decrease (since $H^+(aq)$ ions are produced).

11. (a) The pH in the mouth decreases.
(b) Snacks will decrease the pH more often during the day, and teeth will be exposed to acid attack more often each day.
(c) Alkaline toothpaste will neutralise the acid which attacks teeth.

12. Metal oxides normally dissolve in water to give an alkaline solution. $CrO_3(s)$ however gives an acidic solution.

13. (a) Phosphorus burns in air to give phosphorus oxide. This is a non-metal oxide and will dissolve in water to give an acidic solution.
(b) (i) no effect
(ii) All the oxygen in the air was used up by the smaller piece of phosphorus.

14. (a) $H^+(aq)$ and $OH^-(aq)$
(b) the solution
(c) The concentration of hydroxide ions decreases.

15. (a) Pure water contains equal numbers of $H^+(aq)$ and $OH^-(aq)$ ions and is therefore neutral (an acid contains more $H^+(aq)$ than $OH^-(aq)$ ions).
(b) (i) As water is added, the concentration of $H^+(aq)$ ions decreases and the pH increases.
(ii) 7
(iii) The acid can be only be diluted so that it is almost pure water, but there can never be an excess of $OH^-(aq)$ ions.

16. (a) It increases.
(b) As the concentration of the carbon dioxide increases, the pH decreases.
(c) As the concentration of the carbon dioxide increases, the concentration of $H^+(aq)$ ions increases, and the pH will therefore decrease.

17.

Acid solutions	pH	Alkali solutions	pH	Neutral solutions	pH
vinegar	4	bicarbonate of soda	9	washing-up liquid	7
cola drink	3	drain cleaner	14		
lemon juice	3	milk	8		
		indigestion pill	10		
		window cleaner	12		

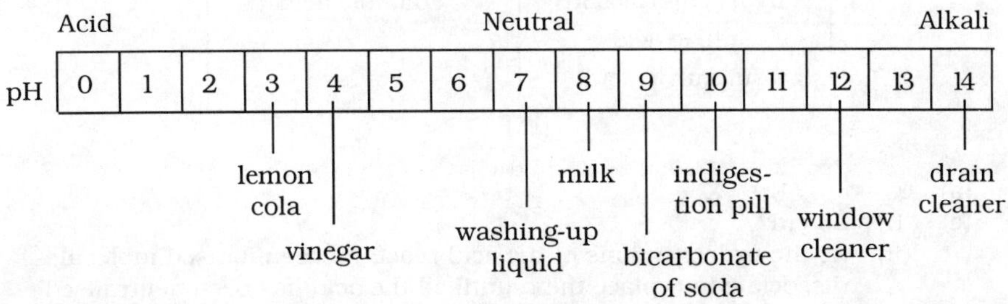

18. (a) 0.4 kg (b) 1.3 kg (c) 24 kg

19. (a) 2 (b) 210 °C

20. (a) **C** (22.5 cm^3 of chlorine per cm^3 of bleach)
(b) Poisonous chlorine gas would be given off when the bleach reacts with acid.

Exercise 3.2 Concentration

1. (a) 0.5 mol (b) 0.1 mol (c) 0.01 mol (d) 0.5 mol (e) 0.5 mol

2. (a) 10 mol l^{-1} (b) 2 mol l^{-1} (c) 0.2 mol l^{-1}
(d) 2 mol l^{-1} (e) 2 mol l^{-1}

3. (a) 2 l (b) 2 l (c) 0.05 l (d) 5 l (e) 0.25 l

4. (a) 4 g (b) 2.8 g (c) 10.6 g (d) 0.345 g (e) 33 g
(f) 8.2 g

5. (a) 0.097 mol l^{-1} (b) 0.25 mol l^{-1} (c) 0.8 mol l^{-1}
(d) 0.4 mol l^{-1} (e) 0.25 mol l^{-1} (f) 0.005 mol l^{-1}

Exercise 3.3 Strong and weak acids and bases

1. (a) (i) A concentrated acid contains a large quantity of pure acid dissolved to make a relatively small volume of solution.
A dilute acid contains a small quantity of pure acid dissolved to make a relatively large volume of solution.
(ii) A weak acid contains a large proportion of unionised molecules of acid in aqueous solution.
A strong acid is almost fully ionised in solution.
(b) (i) for example, ethanoic acid, citric acid
(ii) for example, hydrochloric acid, sulphuric acid, nitric acid
(c) (i) The concentration of hydrogen ions decreases in proportion to the volume of the acid solution.
(ii) The number of hydrogen ions is almost unchanged.

2.

Strong acids	Weak acids
hydrochloric acid	ethanoic acid
nitric acid	
sulphuric acid	

3. (a) **X** (b) **X**
(c) (i) 25 cm^3
(ii) As the hydrogen ions of the acid react, more unionised molecules dissociate to replace them until all the acid has been neutralised.

4. (a) **A**
   (b) The pH of solution **A** is lower, therefore the concentration of hydrogen ions is greater. The solution therefore has a greater degree of ionisation and is stronger.

5. (a) $NH_3(g) + H_2O(l) \rightleftharpoons NH_4^+(aq) + OH^-(aq)$

   (b) Unless the solutions are at the same concentration it is not possible to make fair comparisons of the relative concentrations of $OH^-(aq)$ ions in solution since the potential number of ions which could form should be the same.
   (c) Sodium hydroxide is a strong base and is fully ionised in solution.
   The concentration of $OH^-(aq)$ is high and the pH of the solution is also high.
   Since ammonia is a weak base, the concentration of $OH^-(aq)$ in solution is much lower and the pH is lower.
   Since sodium hydroxide is fully ionised, the overall number of ions in solution is high and therefore the conductivity is high, whereas ammonia solution contains relatively few ions and has much lower conductivity.
   Both solutions will be neutralised by the same volume of acid, because the addition of acid causes the equilibrium in ammonia solution to move producing more $OH^-(aq)$ ions in the solution until all the ammonia molecules have dissociated.

Exercise 3.4 Reactions of acids

1. (a) In a neutralisation reaction an acid and an alkali react to form a salt and water.
   (b) It increases until it reaches 7.
   (c) It decreases until it reaches 7.
   (d) $H^+(aq) + OH^-(aq) \rightarrow H_2O(l)$

2. (a) Lime is an alkali and neutralises the acidity of the soil.
   (b) Indigestion is caused by excess acidity in the stomach. Milk of magnesia is an alkali, and can neutralise this excess acidity.

3. (a) The scale is an alkali and reacts with the vinegar which is an acid,
   (b) neutralisation
   (c) water

4. Lithium hydroxide is an alkali and will react with carbon dioxide, an acidic oxide, to form lithium carbonate and water, removing it from the atmosphere.

5. (a) (i) carbon dioxide
   (ii) Bubble the gas through limewater; turns milky.
   (b) (i) calcium sulphate, carbon dioxide and water
   (ii) sodium nitrate, carbon dioxide and water
   (c) $2H^+(aq) + CO_3^{2-}(aq) \rightarrow CO_2(g) + H_2O(l)$

6. (a) (i) hydrogen (ii) It "pops" when tested with a lighted splint.
(b) (i) calcium chloride and hydrogen
(ii) magnesium sulphate and hydrogen
(c) $2H^+(aq) + 2e^- \rightarrow H_2(g)$

7. (a) neutralisation (b) It increases. (c) by filtration

8. (a) carbon dioxide (b) It is a carbonate.

9. Add dilute hydrochloric acid to both solids. The solid which gives off a gas (which turns limewater milky) will be sodium carbonate.

10. (a) To dilute the acid to make it less corrosive.
(b) (i) neutralisation (ii) carbon dioxide

11. (a) for example, the burning of fossil fuels
(b) acid rain
(c) for example, damages forests, damages lakes, damages buildings
(d) (i) nitrogen dioxide
(ii) car exhaust fumes

12. (a) (i) metal chloride and water
(ii) neutralisation
(b) Add the tablet to a small quantity of dilute hydrochloric acid to which a few drops of Universal indicator have been added. As the acid is neutralised, the colour of the indicator will change from red to green.

13. (a) **A** and **B**
(b) The effluent from the explosives factory is acidic and will neutralise the alkaline effluent from the soap factory.

14. (a) Carbon dioxide is an acidic gas and reacts with potassium hydroxide (an alkali) to give potassium carbonate and water.
(b)

15. John would treat the mixture with dilute hydrochloric acid (or dilute sulphuric acid). The copper oxide would react to form copper(II) chloride (copper(II) sulphate), but the copper metal would not dissolve. This mixture would then be filtered. Copper would remain in the filter paper and copper(II) chloride solution (copper(II) sulphate solution) and unreacted acid would pass through. The copper would then be washed with pure water to remove any remaining solution and dried in a warm oven.

16. (a) (i), (ii), (vi), (ix), (x)
(b) (i), (vi), (x)

17. (a)

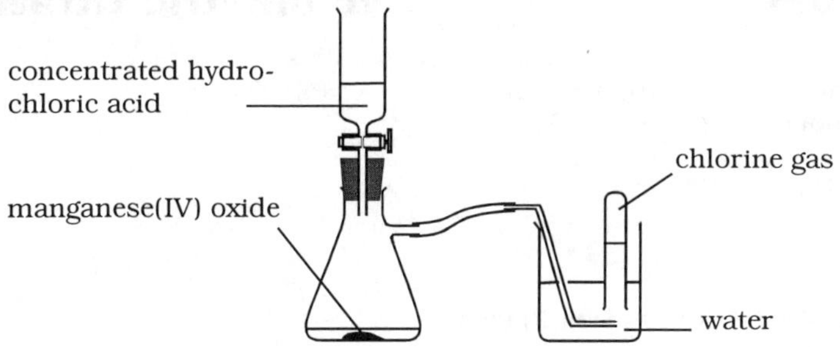

18. (a)

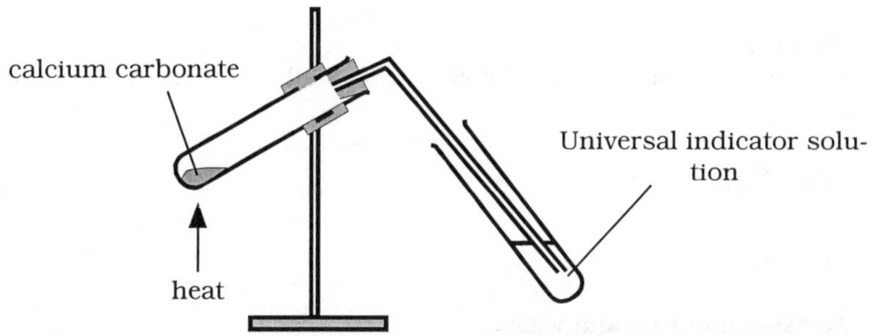

(b) orange

19. (a) Neutralisation is an exothermic reaction.
(b)

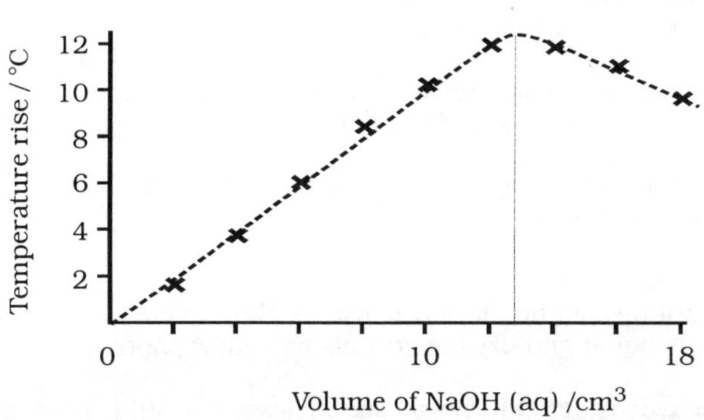

(c) 12.7 cm^3
(d) The volume of sodium hydroxide solution required would be less.

Exercise 3.5 Volumetric titrations

1. (a) 100 cm^3 (b) 0.25 mol l^{-1} (c) 5 cm^3
   (d) 0.16 mol l^{-1} (e) 0.36 mol l^{-1}

2. D, G, A, H, F, E

3. 0.089 mol l^{-1}

4. (a) To dissolve the iron as iron(II) ions.
   (b) hydrogen
   (c) (i) 0.0030 mol (ii) 0.85 g

5. (a) 10 cm^3
   (b) Evaporate the solution until concentrated, allow to cool and crystallise.

Exercise 3.6 Salts

1. (iii), (iv), (viii), (xii)

2. (a) potassium nitrate and water
   (b) sodium sulphate and water
   (c) lithium chloride and water

3. (a) sodium hydroxide and hydrochloric acid
   (b) potassium hydroxide and sulphuric acid
   (c) barium hydroxide and nitric acid

4. (a) magnesium sulphate, carbon dioxide, water
   (b) potassium nitrate, carbon dioxide, water

5. (a) aluminium chloride, hydrogen
   (b) zinc sulphate, hydrogen

6. (a) hydrochloric acid
   (b) Evaporate until the solution is concentrated, allow to cool and crystallise. Pour off excess liquid and dry the crystals on a filter paper.

7. (a) (i) sodium hydroxide (ii) magnesium chloride (iii) hydrogen
   (b) neutralisation

8. (a) copper oxide, dilute sulphuric acid
   (b) neutralisation
   (c) copper(II) ion

9. (a) 2 (b) potassium chromate

10. Jack could use an excess of copper(II) oxide and filter off unused oxide because it is insoluble in water. Jill's reactants and products are all soluble in water.

11. (a) $OH^-(aq) + H^+(aq) \rightarrow H_2O(l)$
(b) $OH^-(aq) + H^+(aq) \rightarrow H_2O(l)$
(c) $CO_3^{2-}(aq) + 2H^+(aq) \rightarrow H_2O(l) + CO_2(g)$

12. (a) Artificial fertilisers added to the soil.
(b) Nitrates taken up by growing plants.
(c) It causes abundant plant growth in rivers and streams which can reduce the water flow rate and oxygen levels.

13. (a) ammonia - NH_3 ammonium nitrate - NH_4NO_3
(b) nitric acid

14. (a) potassium hydroxide (b) water
(c) neutralisation
(d) very soluble in water, provide a nutrient which can be absorbed directly by plants

15. (a) To neutralise acidic soils which do not sustain the growth of many plants.
(b) The lime and fertiliser react releasing ammonia into the air. This removes the fixed nitrogen from the fertiliser and it is not longer available as a plant nutrient.

$$(NH_4)_2SO_4 + Ca(OH)_2 \rightarrow CaSO_4 + 2NH_3 + 2H_2O$$

16. (a) iron(II) ions
(b) sulphuric acid

17.

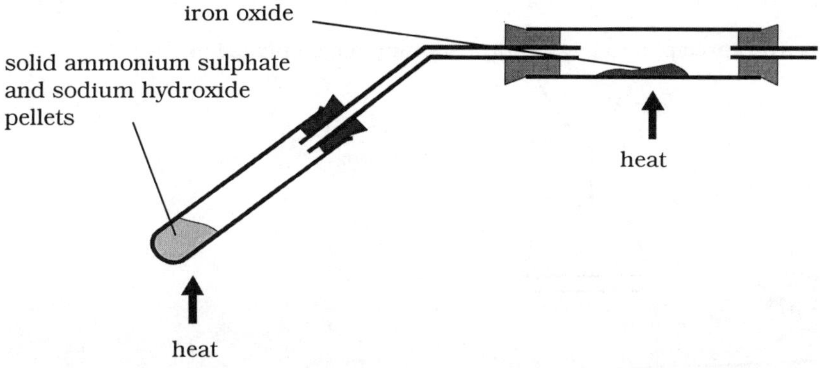

18. (a) 1935
(b) Use of artificial fertilisers is increasing.
(c) potassium nitrate
(d) It is insoluble in water.

19. (a) Ammonia reacts with hydrogen chloride to produce ammonium chloride.
(b) Ammonia gas molecules move (approx 2×) faster than hydrogen chloride molecules.

Exercise 3.7 Precipitation

1. (a) precipitation
   (b) (i) barium sulphate (ii) calcium sulphate (iii) silver chloride

2. (a) (i) magnesium nitrate, sodium carbonate
   (ii) Mix solutions of magnesium nitrate and sodium carbonate. Filter off magnesium carbonate precipitate, wash with pure water and allow to dry.

3. (a) barium sulphate (b) precipitation (c) filtration

4. (a) silver chloride (b) Potassium chloride is soluble in water.

5. (a) sodium sulphate, barium chloride
   (b) sodium chloride, barium chloride (unused), sodium sulphate (unused)
   (c) Because barium sulphate is insoluble, it cannot be absorbed into the bloodstream from the digestive system, and cannot act as a poison.

6. (a) $Ag^+(aq) + Cl^-(aq) \rightarrow Ag^+Cl^-(s)$
   (b) $Cu^{2+}(aq) + 2OH^-(aq) \rightarrow Cu^{2+}(OH^-)_2(s)$
   (c) $Ba^{2+}(aq) + SO_4{}^{2-}(aq) \rightarrow Ba^{2+}SO_4{}^{2-}(s)$
   (d) $Cu^{2+}(aq) + CO_3{}^{2-}(aq) \rightarrow Cu^{2+}CO_3{}^{2-}(s)$

7. (a) chloride ions (and excess barium ions)
   (b) $Ba^{2+}(aq) + CO_3{}^{2-}(aq) \rightarrow Ba^{2+}CO_3{}^{2-}(s)$

8. (a) (i) precipitation (ii) sodium ion, sulphate ion
   (b)

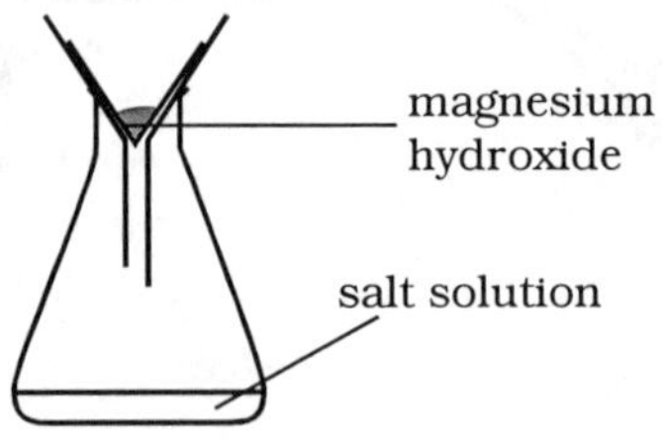

Exercise 3.8 The electrochemical series

1. (a) To allow ions to move between the electrodes, completing the circuit.
   (b) from iron to copper
   (c) It would increase.

2. Magnesium is more reactive than copper and displaces copper ions from copper sulphate solution. The magnesium ribbon breaks up as magnesium atoms form magnesium ions, losing electrons to the blue copper ions which are removed from the solution as brown copper metal.
   Magnesium is less reactive than sodium and cannot displace sodium ions from solution.

3. (a) from tin to copper (b) sodium chloride
   (c) It is insoluble and the ions would be unable to move.
   (d) higher

4. (a) from copper to silver
   (b) Copper is more reactive than silver and forms its ions more easily.

5. (a) **A** - magnesium chloride solution, **B** - magnesium,
   C - copper sulphate solution, **D** - copper
   (b) (i) a salt bridge (ii) To complete the circuit.
   (iii) Sodium chloride solution contains freely moving ions; sugar solution is covalent.

6. (a) from zinc to copper (b) The reading would be higher.
   (c) The zinc rod would become smaller. The blue colour of the copper sulphate solution wouldbecome lighter.

7. When the copper coin is placed in silver nitrate solution a displacement reaction can occur. Silver is deposited on the coin since copper is a more reactive metal than silver.
   Copper is less reactive than sodium, therefore sodium ions cannot be displaced from solution and no reaction occurs.

8. (a) Ethanol is a covalent liquid. Ions are not available to move between the electrodes.
   (b) The reading will be lower.

9. (a) **S** (b) **S**> Zn> **R**> **T**

10. (a) (i) from magnesium to copper
    (ii) Magnesium is a more reactive metal than copper.
    (b) for example, silver, gold
    (c) The reading would be lower.
    (d) (i) It would become zero.
    (ii) Sugar is a covalent substance. No ions would be available to move between the electrodes.

11. (a) To the copper can and the zinc rod.
(b) Ions would be unable to move between the zinc chloride solution and the copper chloride solution.

12. (a) electrochemical series
(b) Magnesium is below sodium in the electrochemical series and is unable to displace sodium ions from solution.
(c) (i) 0.1V (ii) – 0.8V (iii) magnesium

13. (a) Metal **X** would displace copper(II) ions from copper(II) sulphate solution.
(b) no reaction

14. (a) It is a very reactive metal which is easily oxidised.
(b) To allow ions to flow between the electrodes.
(c) Water would react with the lithium to produce hydrogen gas which would make the battery explode.

15. (a)

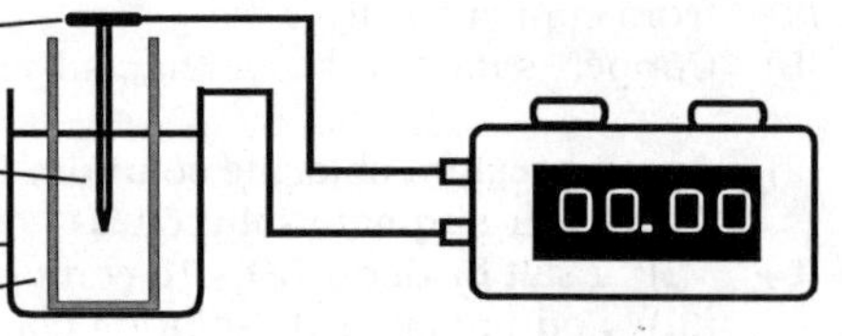

(b) (i) brown
(ii) Copper(II) ions are reduced to copper by more active iron metal.
(c) Aluminium reacts with oxygen in the air to form a tough, water resistant coating of aluminium oxide which prevents the aluminium underneath from reacting.

Exercise 3.9 Redox reactions

1. (a) (i) reaction (ii) no reaction (iii) reaction
(iv) no reaction (v) no reaction (vi) no reaction

(b) (i) $Mg(s) \rightarrow Mg^{2+}(aq) + 2e^-$ oxidation
$Cu^{2+}(aq) + 2e^- \rightarrow Cu(s)$ reduction
(iii) $Zn(s) \rightarrow Zn^{2+}(aq) + 2e^-$ oxidation
$Ag^+(aq) + e^- \rightarrow Ag(s)$ reduction

2. (a) **P** - iron, tin **Q** - aluminium
(b) (i) blue
(ii) $Cu(s) \rightarrow Cu^{2+}(aq) + 2e^-$ (oxidation)

3. (a) (i) It is oxidised to form $Zn^{2+}(aq)$ ions.
(ii) $Cu^{2+}(aq)$ ions are reduced to copper metal atoms.
(iii) Colour changes from blue to colourless.

(b) $Zn(s) \rightarrow Zn^{2+}(aq) + 2e^-$ (oxidation)
$Cu^{2+}(aq) + 2e^- \rightarrow Cu(s)$ (reduction)

4. (a) from magnesium to metal **X**
   (b) $Mg(s) \rightarrow Mg^{2+}(aq) + 2e^-$
   (c) the magnesium
   (d) $\mathbf{X}^+(aq) + e^- \rightarrow \mathbf{X}(s)$

5. (a) reduction
   (b) from electrode **A** to electrode **B**.
   (c) iodine
   (d) $2I^-(aq) \rightarrow I_2(aq) + 2e^-$

6. (a) displacement
   (b) $Ag^+(aq) + e^- \rightarrow Ag(s)$
   (c) Platinum is less reactive than silver.

7. (a) oxidation
   (b) from **B** to **A**
   (c) Iron(III) ions gain one electron and are reduced to form iron(II) ions.
   (d) $Fe^{3+}(aq) + e^- \rightarrow Fe^{2+}(aq)$

8. (a) **X** is sodium sulphite solution; **Y** is bromine solution.
   (b) To allow ions to move between solution **X** and solution **Y**.
   (c) $Br_2(aq) + 2e^- \rightarrow 2Br^-(aq)$
   (d) The bromine solution would be decolourised.

9. (a) redox
   (b) (i) $Br_2(aq) + 2e^- \rightarrow 2Br^-(aq)$
   (ii) $SO_3^{2-}(aq) + H_2O(l) \rightarrow SO_4^{2-}(aq) + 2H^+(aq) + 2e^-$

10. (a) (i) electrode **A** (ii) electrode **B**
    (b) $SO_3^{2-}(aq) + H_2O(l) \rightarrow SO_4^{2-}(aq) + 2H^+(aq) + 2e^-$
    (c) Positive ions move through the salt bridge towards electrode **B**, and negative ions move through the salt bridge to electrode **A**.

11. (a) $Ni^{2+}(aq) + 2e^- \rightarrow Ni(s)$
    (b) reduction
    (c) negative electrode

12. (a) electrolysis
    (b) reduction
    (c) $2Cl^-(aq) \rightarrow Cl_2(aq) + 2e^-$
    (d) Avoids shutting down the cell to replace the sodium chloride solution, and makes the process more efficient.

13. (a) oxidation
    (b) positive
    (c) increases
    (d) $Cu^{2+}(aq) + 2e^- \rightarrow Cu(s)$

14. (a) $Cu^{2+}(aq) + 2e^- \rightarrow Cu(s)$
(b) $2Cl^-(aq) \rightarrow Cl_2(aq) + 2e^-$

15. (a) reduction
(b) It will increase to a value greater than 7 since there is an increase in the concentration of OH^- (aq) ions in the solution.

Exercise 3.10 Metals and metal ores

1. (a) lithium, sodium and potassium
(b) Very reactive with air and water at ordinary temperatures.

2. (a) potassium permanganate
(b) Oxygen gas reacts with the heated metal. The reactivity of different metals is judged by the heat energy evolved as the metals react.

3. (a) The gas burns with a "pop".
(b) The reaction is so exothermic that the temperaure of the sodium rises above its melting point.
(c) potassium

4. (a) They occur uncombined in the Earth's crust, and do not require to be extracted from their ores.
(b) They are reactive metals and can only be extracted from their molten compounds by the use of electricity.

5. (a) Uncombined - these metals are found in nature as elements.
Ores - metals compounds from which it is economical to extract the metallic element.
(b) gold, silver
(c) They are very unreactive metals.
(d) iron, lead, copper

6. (a) for example, silver oxide (b) sodium oxide

7. (a) blast furnace
(b) (i) carbon + oxygen → carbon dioxide
(ii) carbon + carbon dioxide → carbon monoxide
(iii) iron oxide + carbon monoxide → iron + carbon dioxide

8. (a) **Y** > **X** > **Z**
(b) **Y** - potassium, sodium, lithium, calcium, magnesium, aluminium
X - zinc, iron, tin, lead, copper.
Z - mercury, silver

9. (a) **L** is a very unreactive metal.
(b) Heat the metal oxides with carbon. The oxide which is most easily reduced to the metal is the less reactive metal.

10. (a) reduction
    (b) Calcium is a very reactive metal. Its oxide can be reduced to the metal only by electrolysis of the melt.

11. (a) The melting point of uranium(IV) fluoride is greater than 100 °C.
    The melting point of uranium(IV) fluoride is less than 1600 °C.
    (b) less reactive

12. (a) (i) **W** and **Y** are more reactive than **X** and **Z**.
    (ii) **Z** is less reactive than **W**, **X** and **Y**.
    (b) **W** > **Y** > **X** > **Z**
    (c) **W** - calcium, **Y** - magnesium, **X** - copper, **Z** - silver

13. (a) (i) **C** is more reactive than **A**.
    (ii) **B** is more reactive than **D**.
    (iii) **D** is more reactive than **A**.
    (iv) **C** is more reactive than **B**.
    (b) **C** > **B** > **D** > **A**

14. (a) (i) **A** > **M** > **E**, **T**, **L**
    (ii) **T** > **E**
    (iii) **M**, **A**, **L** > **E**, **T**
    (iv) **M**, **A**, **L** > **E**, **T**
    (b) **A** > **M** > **L** > **T** > **E**
    (c) **E**

15.

Metal	**Date of discovery**	**Properties**	**Use**
gold	earliest times	soft	jewellery, coins
copper	4000 B.C.	unreactive good conductor	water pipes electrical wiring
iron	1000 B.C.	hard	cars, machinery, ships, railway lines
aluminium	1825 A.D.	light corrosion resistant	aircraft, cooking foil window frames, milk bottle tops,

16. (a) The hardness increases as the percentage of carbon increases.
    (b) high hardness, low strength

17. (a)

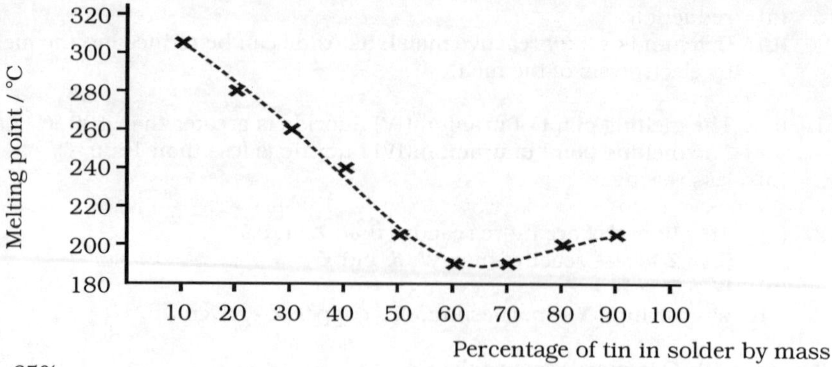

(b) 65%

(c) Lead from the solder may dissolve in the drinking water and make it poisonous.

18. (a) gas

(b) It is a very active metal which will react with air or water at ordinary temperatures.

19. **A**

20. The metals do not react with air under normal conditions.
At very high temperatures the metals react with oxygen in the air to form their oxides.

21. **B**, **C**

22. (a) Sodium has a much lower melting point than iron.

(b) The boiling point of sodium is much higher than the boiling point of water, and can be used at higher temperatures without gas forming and building up a dangerous pressure, or sodium is a better conductor of heat, or sodium is very reactive.

Exercise 3.11 Corrosion

1. (a) The oxidation of the surface of a metal to form a compound by exposure to the atmosphere.

(b) rusting

(c)

Substances which corrode	Substances which do not corrode
magnesium zinc sodium aluminium calcium	glass sandstone sulphur calcium carbonate plastic

2. (a) oxygen and water
   (b) They are (initially) oxidised to iron(II) ions.

3. It increases the rate of corrosion.

4. (a) The more intense the blue colour formed in the same time, the faster the rate of corrosion.
   (b) Salt dissolves in the water forming the cell electrolyte which allows iron(II) ions to form more easily.
   Glucose is covalent. In solution it produces no ions to accelerate the rusting process.

5. (a) **A**
   (b) Tin is less reactive than iron and accepts electrons from the iron. This allows the iron to form its ions more easily and accelerates rusting.

6. (a) The salt dissolved in sea water increases the rate of corrosion.
   (b) Magnesium is more reactive than iron, and sacrificially protects the iron.
   (c) The copper connections will increase the rate of corrosion of the iron because iron sacrificially protects the less reactive copper.
   (d) The paint forms a protective layer preventing moisture and oxygen from reaching the iron surface.
   (e) The copper will increase the rate of corrosion of the lead, and both weaken the joint and increase the formation of toxic lead compounds in the water.
   (f) Electrons are passed to the car body and prevent the iron forming iron(II) ions.
   (g) Magnesium will protect the iron sacrificially, but copper will accelerate the corrosion of the iron.

7. (a) ferroxyl indicator
   (b) Iron which has been coated by dipping it into molten zinc.
   (c) The zinc is more reactive than the iron and protects iron sacrificially.

8. (a) galvanising
   (b) Even when scratched the zinc continues to protect the iron by sacrificial protection. A scratched tin coating will accelerate the rusting of iron since iron is more reactive than tin and sacrificially protects the tin layer.

9. (a) nail **B**
   (b) Magnesium is more reactive than iron and corrodes in preference to the iron. Electrons are transferred to the iron, slowing down the formation of iron(II) ions.
   (c) Experiment 1 illustrates cathodic protection which is used to protect iron piers, jetties and the bodies of cars.
   Experiment 2 illustrates sacrificial protection which is used to protect the hulls of steel ships and underground pipes.

10. Sacrificial protection. Bolt blocks of magnesium to the steel structure. The magnesium corrodes in preference to the iron and passes electrons to the the steel structure preventing the formation of iron(II) ions.

11. (a) Physical protection provided by the copper would be better since copper is a less reactive metal than zinc and will corrode more slowly.
    (b) Electrochemical protection provided by the copper would be much worse than that provided by zinc, because copper is less reactive than iron and electrons would flow from the iron to the copper increasing the rate of rusting of the iron.

12. (a) **Y** is more reactive.
    (b) **Y**

13. (a) electroplating
    (b) The iron surface is covered by a layer of less reactive metal which corrodes only slowly itself; it prevents air and moisture from reaching the iron surface.

14. The low temperature slows down the chemical reactions of the rusting process or there is less water vapour in the air at temperatures below freezing point.

15. (a) The plastic layer prevents air and moisture reaching the iron surface.
    (b) Chromium is less reactive than iron.

16. (a) oxidation
    (b) (i) $Fe(s) \rightarrow Fe^{2+}(aq) + 2e^-$ (ii) $Zn(s) \rightarrow Zn^{2+}(aq) + 2e^-$
    (iii) $Mg(s) \rightarrow Mg^{2+}(aq) + 2e^-$ (iv) $Al(s) \rightarrow Al^{3+}(aq) + 3e^-$
    (c) $Fe^{2+}(aq) \rightarrow Fe^{3+}(aq) + e^-$
    (d) $O_2(g) + 2H_2O(l) + 4e^- \rightarrow 4OH^-(aq)$

17. Carbon dioxide from the atmosphere dissolves in moisture on the surface of the nail to produce a slightly acidic solution which speeds up the rusting process. Sodium hydroxide (an alkali) removes the acidic carbon dioxide gas.

18. (a) $Fe(s) \rightarrow Fe^{2+}(aq) + 2e^-$
    $2H^+(aq) + 2e^- \rightarrow H_2(g)$
    (b) The acid mist will dissolve the zinc layer on the surface of the iron very quickly, preventing the zinc from protecting the iron either physically or by sacrificial protection.

19. (a) (i) **B**
    (ii) Tin is an unreactive metal and prevents air and moiture reaching the surface of the iron to make it rust.
    (b) (i) **C**
    (ii) Tin is less reactive than iron. When the iron is exposed, iron passes electrons to the tin allowing the iron to rust more quickly.

20. (a) (i) iron(II) ions
(ii) hydroxide ions
(b) iron/zinc cell - red at iron electrode
iron/tin cell - blue at iron electrode, red at tin elecrode
carbon/iron cell - blue at iron electrode, red at carbon electrode
(c) iron/zinc cell iron - $O_2(g) + 2H_2O(l) + 4e^- \rightarrow 4OH^-(aq)$
zinc - $Zn(s) \rightarrow Zn^{2+}(aq) + 2e^-$
iron/tin cell iron - $Fe(s) \rightarrow Fe^{2+}(aq) + 2e^-$
tin - $O_2(g) + 2H_2O(l) + 4e^- \rightarrow 4OH^-(aq)$
carbon/iron cell iron - $Fe(s) \rightarrow Fe^{2+}(aq) + 2e^-$
carbon - $O_2(g) + 2H_2O(l) + 4e^- \rightarrow 4OH^-(aq)$
(d) zinc to iron, iron to tin, iron to carbon

21. (a) displacement or redox
(b) Copper is less reactive than iron. Electrons flow from iron to copper allowing iron to be oxidised to iron(II) ions more rapidly.

22. Gold is less reactive than mercury, silver or tin. Electrons will therefore flow from the amalgam filling to the gold filling, allowing the metals in the amalgam to oxidise more rapidly.

23. (a) $Cu(s) \rightarrow Cu^{2+}(aq) + 2e^-$
(b) Iron is more reactive than copper and electrons will flow from the iron to the copper, making the iron rust more rapidly but making the copper corrode more slowly.

24. Iron is more reactive than copper and electrons will flow from iron to copper. The nails will rust very rapidly and fail to secure the copper to the hull. With copper nails there will be no corrosion of the nails.

Prescribed Practical Activities

1. Take 20 cm^3 of sodium thiosulphate solution and measure its temperature with a thermometer. Place the beaker on the card with the cross, add 1 cm^3 of acid, stir and start a stopclock. When the cross is obscured, stop the stopclock and measure the temperature of the solution. Record the time taken for the experiment to occur.
Repeat the experiment, but gently warm the sodium thiosulphate solution first. Repeat this for a range of temperature between room temperature and 50 °C. Calculate the average temperature for each experiment and the relative rate by finding the reciprocal of the time taken.
Plot a graph of relative rate against temperature.

2. (a) 2 cm^3, 4cm^3, 6cm^3
(b) Starch indicator turns blue-black when free iodine is formed.

3. The initial and final temperatures of the thiosulphate solution should be measured and the average temperature of the experiment calculated.
The experiment should be carried out repeating the experiment at more than one different temperature.

4. (a) the volume and concentration of the potassium iodide solution
the volume and concentration of starch solution
the total volume of the solution
the container used for the observation of the colour change
(b) The starch turns blue-black.

5. (a)

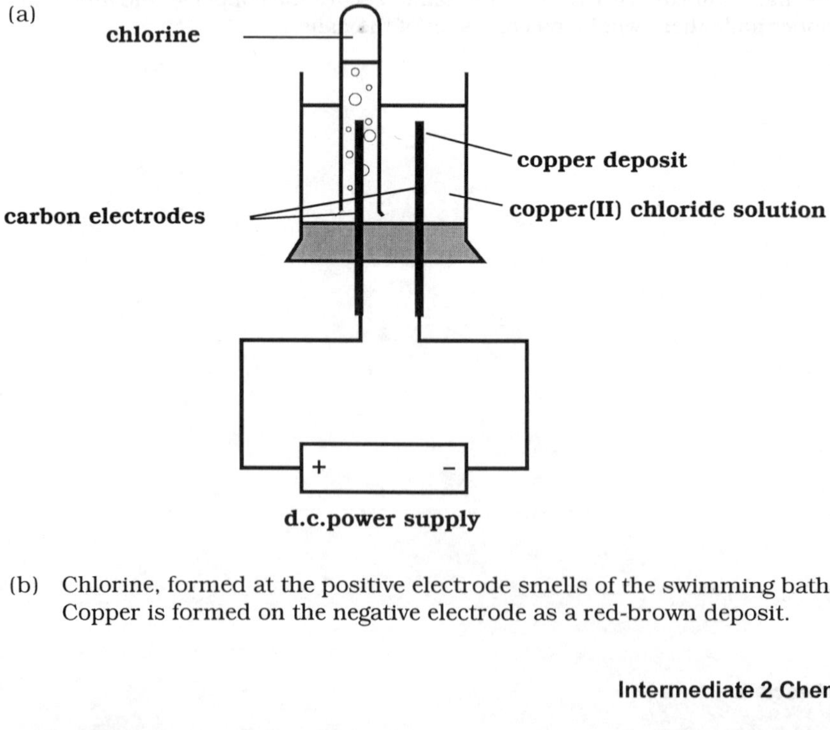

(b) Chlorine, formed at the positive electrode smells of the swimming baths.
Copper is formed on the negative electrode as a red-brown deposit.

6. (a) Add bromine solution and shake. The solution decolourises rapidly in the absence of light.
   (b) The experiment should be carried out in a fume cupboard to avoid the release of toxic fumes of bromine, or a special bottle should be used for the disposal of organic waste.

7. (a)

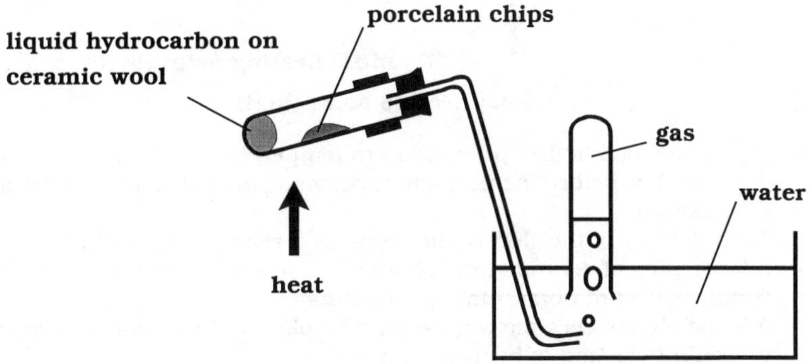

   (b) (i) When heated apparatus is allowed to cool, gases inside the apparatus contract and the pressure inside the apparatus falls below atmospheric pressure. The outside air pressure will force water back along the delivery tube into the hot apparatus which may shatter when the cold water comes into contact with hot glass.
   (ii) Remove the apparatus from the source of heat and from the water by lifting the supporting clamp stand.

8. (a) In the hydrolysis of starch using an enzyme or an acid, the enzyme and acid act as a catalyst.
   (b) Benedict's solution

9. (a) neutralisation ($MgCO_3$) or redox (Mg)
   filtration
   evaporation
   (b) To ensure that there is no unused acid which would be more difficult to remove.

10. (a)

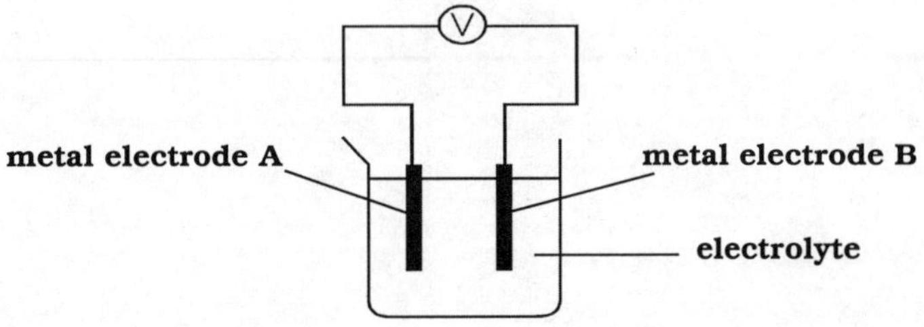

   (b) eg. the concentration of the electrolyte, the temperature of the electrolyte, the nature of the electrolyte
   Accept: the distance apart of the electrodes, the depth of the electrolyte

11. (a)

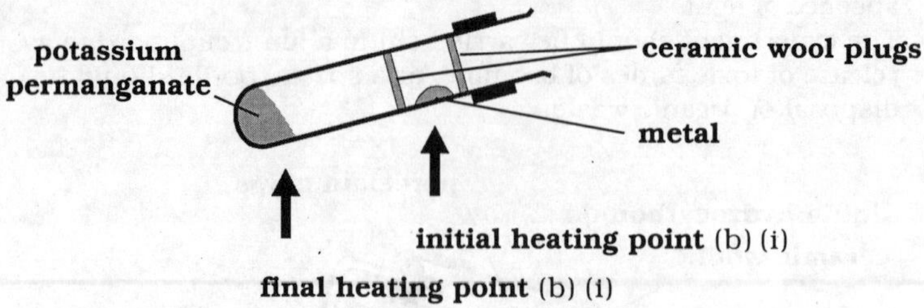

(b) (ii) The metal is first brought up to temperature so that it can react quickly, before the potassium permanganate is heated to release oxygen.

(c) The intensity of the glow of the metal as it reacts with oxygen.

(d) A loose plug of ceramic wool should be used to prevent metal coming into contact with hot potassium permanganate.
A loose plug of ceramic wool should be placed at the mouth of the test tube to prevent ejection of burning material.
The apparatus should be pointed towards a wall to prevent possible injury to nearby people.

12. (a) To act as a control to show that the hydrolysis is very slow in the absence of a catalyst.

(b) (i) dilute mineral acid or enzyme (e.g. amylase)
(ii) 100 °C or 37 °C

(c) Benedict's solution turns from blue-green to give a brick red precipitate.